A PEOPLE PRIMER

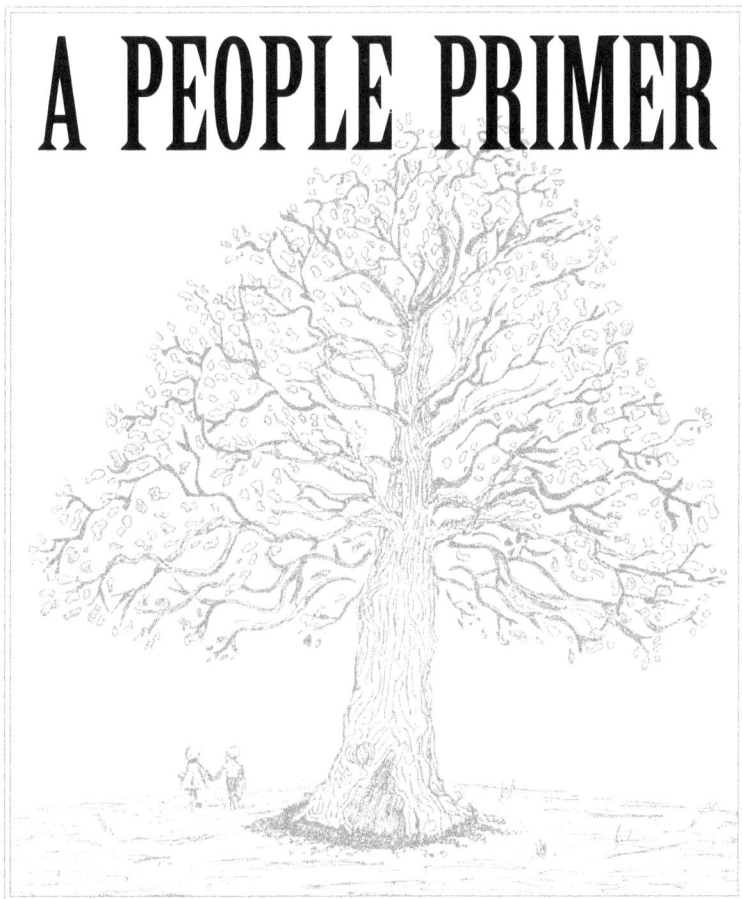

THE NATURE OF LIVING SYSTEMS

SHELLEY ROY

This book

A People Primer
The Nature of Living Systems
can be downloaded from www.livingcontrolsystems.com,
and www.archive.org/details/perceptual-control.
File: PeoplePrimerRoy2025.pdf
For more, search *Perceptual Control Theory*

Dedication

This book is dedicated to my two favorite engineers: My father, **George M. Workman**, who first helped me learn to think in technical terms; and to **William T. Powers**, whose ideas and thinking have brought Perceptual Control Theory to me and the rest of the world. Both humble geniuses who have touched my life.

Publishers Cataloging in Publication:
Roy, Shelley A.W. 1955-
    A People Primer :
        the nature of living systems
    /by Shelley A.W. Roy.
    viii, 226 p. : ill. ; 23 cm.
    Includes bibliographical references.
    978-1-938090-24-0 (softcover, perfect binding)
    1. Psychotherapy.   2 Cognitive therapy. 3. Counseling.
    4. Clinical psychology. 5. Mental health.
    6. Perceptual control theory.   I. Title.

    ⊗ The paper used in this book meets all ANSI standards for
      archival quality paper.

    Published 2008 by newview, Chapel Hill, NC.
    Republished 2025 by Living Control Systems
    Publishing, Menlo Park, CA.
    No changes to text or images.

        Living Control Systems Publishing
        Menlo Park, CA
        www.livingcontrolsystems.com

Acknowledgements

This book would not exist without the encouragement, support, and forward thinking of the following individuals.

The Science Guys who have been patient and provided endless clarification: William T. Powers for his abundant contribution to the field of psychology and Perceptual Control Theory; Rick Marken and Dag Forssell for their plain-speaking technical clarification; Philip J. Runkel for sharing his lifelong study of human behavior; and Tim Carey for his ongoing research and expertise on the Method of Levels.

My colleagues at the International Association for Applied Control Theory for the questions and dialog we have shared on topics associated with Perceptual Control Theory: Barnes Boffey, Shelley Brierley, Sally Berman, Andrea Christopher, Pam Fox, E. Perry Good, Fred Good, Jeff Grumley, Lloyd Klinedinst, Lisa Koester, Larry Larson, Judy McFadden, Denise Pappas, Patti Sebestyen, Glenn Smith, Jane Williams, and all the participants in ACTs I, II and III.

To my friends who allowed me the creative license to create the letters in this book: Alexander Erolin and Anthony Goldston, who inspired me to write endless letters,which gave birth to the idea for the format of this book; Andrea Christopher who asked and asked and asked some more, trying to understand the technical language of PCT and apply it to herself and the children she works with; Daryl Maxwell, whose quiet dedication to helping kids and families and love of music stretched my thinking for non-technical examples; Glenn Smith, who has spent thousands of hours with me trying to understand PCT and taking it to a very special population, the men in orange of Jail North Mecklenburg County, North Carolina; Thomas Lally, a principal who shares my love for the technical and helped me realize how the details of the science can impact an entire school system; Twyla Rice, a fellow seeker, who has helped me keep my body and spirit balanced; Linda Kitzmiller who has reminded me that the past is what got us here, but courage and patience move us forward to a better tomorrow; Dave Voeller, a lifelong friend who has been there for me as a confidant and a supporter and understands my love of the lake better than anyone else I know; Sandra Darling, a leader in education who understands that no matter how difficult improving schools can be, kids are worth it; Tomas Rodriguez, the first reader and supporter of the manuscript, whose unwavering faith in my abilities has sustained me in many a weak moment.

A special thanks to Sally Berman, who waded through all of my mistakes to help me provide a readable manuscript to send to the editor.

Contents

CHAPTER 1

Dear Reader,

Welcome
to taking control
of your life

Dear Reader,

I was walking through a local bookstore the other day looking at the self-help section, and I was thinking that so many things we read about helping ourselves and others are based on Eighteenth Century thinking. We have this box-like mentality — we put people into one box or another and slap labels on the boxes. Most often this is followed by a plethora of strategies or programs that give us a list of specifically what to do and what to say based on what box we are in and what the label is. Examples of this are Phillip C. McGraw's *Life Strategies*, Zig Ziglar's *Success for Dummies*, and John Gray's *Men are From Mars; Women are from Venus: A Practical Guide for Improving Communication and Getting What You Want in Your Relationships*. The Myers-Briggs Type Indicator, which professionals use to place people into one of sixteen boxes, is intended to help people find work that fits them, help people develop more appreciation for individual differences, and suggest how people can use the differences constructively rather than divisively.

At times, this "box and label" type of thinking can provide some important data, but it also ignores a lot of very valuable information. Understanding how to get out of this "box thinking" will help you reach your greatest potential. In short, you need to think about the world and living systems in a whole new way.

The box thinking that many operate under describes living organisms as having clock-like workings, and it contends that if we could just disassemble a person into his component parts — personality type, learning style, ethnicity, gender — and better understand each one, we could reassemble the individual and he would work better. This "if-then" thinking is what advertisers count on when they try to sell you a new product: if you drink milk, then you will look like your favorite TV star. Or if you wear this pair of jeans, then all the girls will chase you. It is what most people think of as just the way life is. Unfortunately, this type of linear logic doesn't take into account how parts work together, how we change over time, or that we are in an ongoing relationship with our ever-changing environment. The bottom line is that we are far greater than the sum of our parts, and are constantly interacting with an increasingly complex world.

Today's physicists have a phrase they use to describe energy: "bundles of potentiality." I think this is a great description of individuals. When I think of people this way, I see each and every person I meet as a bundle of potentiality. Each person is just waiting to tap into some wonderful undiscovered possibilities. I don't see anyone as a label on a box, and I don't think rules and instructions will get any of us very far in taking control of our lives. I think we need to put away the whole "box and label" way of thinking. As my friend Pam Fox said, "It just fills our minds with clutter, and it needs to be packed up and thrown away."

In the book *Season of Life*, author Jeffrey Marx captures a second problem with this type of thinking. At a high school football team's first meeting of the year, a coach explains why players on his team will not be separated and labeled. He says:

> The rest of the world will want to separate you by race, by socioeconomic status, by education levels, by religion, by neighborhoods, by what kind of a car

you drive, by the clothes you wear, by athletic ability. You name it — always gonna be people who want to separate by that stuff. Well, if you let that happen now, then you'll let it happen later. Don't let it happen. If you're one of us, then you won't walk around putting people in boxes. Not now. Not ever. *Because every single one of them has something to offer. Every single one of them is special.* (Emphasis added.)

Later, the coach talks about how this same idea plays out on and off the field. He talks with the team about never letting anyone eat lunch alone, team member or not. The idea here isn't that you're in or our you're out (you're on the team or you're not); it's about realizing that everyone has unique talents and recognizing each person as an individual worthy of belonging to "the team."

When Columbus successfully sailed west to go east, people had to start thinking of the world in a whole new way. The scientists of today are exploring exciting new territory about behavior, and now it is time for us to venture into this new world of thinking. A major change in perspective (Thomas Kuhn called these "paradigm shifts") about how people operate doesn't change the facts of our observations; it changes our perceptions and explanations. This is what I hope to do in this book. I hope to help you fundamentally change your view of behavior to one based on Perceptual Control Theory, a theory of living systems developed by William Powers and first published in the early 1970s.

I want you to clear out the clutter of your understanding of behavior and untangle the mystery of why we behave the way we do. When technology became more advanced and scientists began to observe things they couldn't explain, they had to pack up their old ideas and throw them away. They had to open their minds and explore new theories to explain what they were seeing. Fritjof Capra in *The Web of Life: A New Scientific Understanding to Living Systems* put it this way:

> The exploration of the atomic and subatomic world brought [scientists] in contact with a strange and unexpected reality. In their struggle to grasp this new reality, scientists became painfully aware that their basic concepts, their language, and their whole way of thinking were inadequate to describe atomic phenomena.

Chaos theory, wave theory, nested hierarchies of webs, circular causation, and a whole lot more have become the working vocabulary of today's scientists.

Many people still try to explain the world and what they observe using the same old paradigm. One of the basic explanations of how people operate, based on Newtonian laws of motion, was accepted in the 1700s is still with us today: for every action there is an opposite and equal reaction. The behavioral version was then translated to a postulate that life can be explained using linear cause and effect reasoning. If I dress just right and say just the right thing, I'll be popular. If I hear a phone ringing, I will answer it. If I yell at my children or punish them in other creative ways, I can get them to do what I want. If I reward people for "good" behavior, they will continue to use that behavior. Conversely if I punish them for "bad" behavior, they will stop.

Here is one of the big problems with this type of thinking: if box thinking were true, we could be assured that every time we repeat an action, we will get the exact same results. Have you ever tested this belief? Have you ever done the same thing and gotten a different result? I have. When I was a child I would stick out my tongue at my brother when

I thought he was being especially obnoxious, and he'd answer by sticking his tongue out at me. Then one day I did it, and he grabbed my tongue. When it comes to behavior,

Doing A ≠ Always Getting B

The linear Newtonian way of thinking about the world may hold true when we are talking about creating faster airplanes, constructing buildings, developing computer programs, or doing many other things, but it does not hold true in the same way when we are talking about living organisms. When we apply this linear logic—labeling everything right or wrong, good or bad, positive or negative—to people functioning in a complex environment it simply doesn't work. Like Columbus in his day, we need to see the living world in a new and different way. We need a whole new language to explain behavior, and we need a fundamental change in our thinking. As a friend said to me, "You write to me about systems, the flow in dynamic balance, and webs that grow in interconnections. But boxes, at best I fill them with clutter and dispose of them." I'd like to invite you to dispose of some long held beliefs about human behavior.

This new way of thinking explains why we can't be sure exactly what will happen when we try something. It also leads to one of my favorite truths about living systems: we can produce the same results by taking different actions. This is great news for living things, because we are never ever in exactly the same situation twice. When we shoot free throws in a basketball game, we don't do exactly the same thing every time. But if we are good at this skill, we can get the results we want more often, whether we are in double overtime or in practice. That's what I'm hoping for you. I'm hoping that by reading this book, by better understanding

PCT, you'll find that even when you're dog-tired, your actions will be more effective at bringing about the desired results. Are you ready to pack up the clutter?

Doing A, C, or D may get you B

In this book, we are going to explore a scientific theory of human behavior. Bill Powers states that PCT is the only theory that can be simulated successfully and matched to specific human behavior. Other basic theories are simply assumed to be true without proof or demonstration. I'm going to try to keep the discussion simple and useful. At the end of each chapter, there is an "In a nutshell" section to summarize a few key principles and ideas. This is a tough task because what seems simple gets very complicated when it comes to thinking about people and their behavior. Understanding the theory and putting its principles into action also takes time and practice. All of us have experienced the "wait time" needed to make a skill or a theory our own. The idea of walking seems simple now, but before you could do it, you spent a lot of time falling down, getting up, falling down, and getting up again. We're reminded of this every time we watch a baby learning to walk. If we watch two babies, we'll see that they will not learn to walk in the same way. Learning PCT demonstrates the same principle; everyone will go about it just a little bit differently. That's an exciting part of life, learning how to get the same result by different means!

Here's a little sample of PCT thinking: when you were learning to walk, in PCT terms you were learning how to control a set of perceptions. Saying it this way may sound strange to you, but PCT developer Bill Powers is a systems engineer (not the train kind), and the language of PCT can get technical. For some of you, this may be the most difficult part of learning a new way of thinking. Learning PCT is a lot like learning a new language. Both require a whole lot of practice and patience.

Learning a new language also requires understanding or relearning the meaning of words. Much of our K-12 educational system is about learning the meaning of different words. When you were young, you learned a specific meaning for the word "light." For most of you, the meaning was connected to a lamp or a bulb hanging in the ceiling. Now you have a lot of different meanings for the word. Take a minute and think of how many ways you could use "light" and how many different meanings the word has. Here are some examples: "Come on baby *light* my fire." or "That guy is really a *light*weight." Today you have a deeper understanding of this word. The good news is that once you really understand PCT terminology, you've surmounted one of the biggest hurdles.

When you began to study different content areas in school, did it seem as if each one had its own language? As you learned more and got "smarter," did you realize some languages and ideas could cross over? Think about the word "parallel." It is important in math, in physical education, in language arts, in art, in industrial technology, and so on. In each of these different subjects, we learned about the concept of "parallel," and along the way, it made sense. For me, parallel first made sense in math. I understood what parallel lines were, and it wasn't until I got out of college and had a master's degree that I finally began to realize what my language arts teacher meant by parallel structure. Even now, just because I understand it, doesn't mean I can always apply it correctly. In fact, that's why I have a wonderful editor. In this book, I've tried to provide a lot of examples of PCT principles in different fields of interest. Somewhere along the way I'm hoping the words and the theory will make sense to you in the context of your life experiences.

Something else you need to remember is how words change meaning over time. A popular Tim McGraw country song illustrates this:

> Back when a hoe was a hoe
> Coke was a coke
> And crack's what you were doing
> When you were cracking jokes
> Back when a screw was a screw
> The wind was all that blew
> And when you said I'm down with that
> Well it meant you had the flu.

Understanding words and language leads to better understanding of ourselves and others. The other day, my son asked me if he could borrow my whip. At first I thought, "What do you mean? I don't own a leather strap with a handle." Then I realized that, because he had just gotten his driver's license, he wanted to borrow my car.

As you investigate PCT, some of the terms used will sound familiar to you, but to understand the theory you must be sure you understand how I am using the terms, and what I mean by them. The language of PCT is very precise. The words will sound familiar, and this will give you a general idea of what they mean, but remember that the PCT meaning may be a little different than your present understanding of the word. And, even though you understand the words and their meanings, it isn't always easy to "do PCT" — to act in congruence with PCT rather than opposing its fundamental principles.

I hope this book is going to help you clear the clutter out of your thinking, change the way you see people, and change your explanation of behavior. Are you ready to explore this new understanding of behavior? Are you up for the adventure of taking control of your life? Are you ready to think about living systems, the flow in dynamic balance, and webs that grow in interconnections? Are you willing to take baby step, just as you did when you learned to walk, knowing that if you keep at it, you'll soon be running a four-minute mile?

In deciding on the format for this book, I thought it might help if you could read selected letters that I wrote to some of the people in my life as I tried to help them better understand Perceptual Control Theory. I thought this format might be a lot more fun to read, and I know it's been fun to write. After all, this book is about people. So I've written a series of letters, some based on actual letters, and others based on conversations I've had. I have, however, changed most of the names of those I'm writing to.

Throughout the book, I am going to encourage you to test out the theory for yourself by taking baby steps to apply the theory. I want you to try a few new ways of thinking and a few new basic principles from which to operate. I'm not going to give you a list of rules and strategies; I'm not going to tell you what to do (*When you are talking to someone look them in the eye.*) or what to say (*Always use "I" statements.*) in specific situations. I'm going to sprinkle some ideas based on core behavioral principles throughout the book. (For example, *Pull, don't push.*) I hope these will serve like closet organizers, providing you with cubbies, containers, and bars for storing your new collection of actions.

Here's the first idea I'd like you to think about: *Ask, don't tell.* Try it out in the next couple of days, and see if it makes a difference. I'll give you an example: as I was writing this, my son Duncan walked in to show me a picture he had painted for his art class. I was about to tell him, "I'm so proud of you, you did an excellent job!" Instead, I stopped myself and asked, "Are you proud of yourself?" He beamed and answered, "Yeah, I am." Notice that I not only *asked* rather than *told*, but I also *pulled* the information from him rather than *pushed* it into him. Later we will take a look at more effective questions, but this is a good way to start.

I also suggest that you talk with others who are reading this book. Listening to and discussing with others what you and they are learning can enrich the experience for everyone. And remember to be patient with yourself.

Look within!

In a nutshell

- This book is about fundamentally changing the way we understand behavior.

- This new understanding of behavior is Perceptual Control Theory, originated by William T. Powers.

- Learning PCT is much like learning a new language; it requires patience, practice, and an examination of the use and meaning of words.

- Learning PCT can help you take more effective control of your life.

- Learning PCT leads to the understanding that you have very little control over other living systems. Understanding this principle will greatly relieve stress in your life.

CHAPTER 2

Dear Julius,

Basically,

it's all

about you

In this chapter, I address my first letter to a recent friend of mine. Julius is presently working as a security officer for an international relief organization. Prior to this he was a career military man. He is dedicated to martial arts and loves music. His work takes him around the world. He always carries his instruments along with him to keep him company as he travels for months at a time.

After looking at my website, Julius started asking me about a course I teach called Inside Out Leadership. During his military career he had been involved in many military leadership programs. The basis of the Inside Out Leadership course is Perceptual Control Theory. When I started to explain the ideas behind the course, he became very interested in PCT. This letter reflects some of our first correspondence about the topic.

I hope you learn it's all about you!

Dear Julius,

W hen I talked with you last, you asked if I would explain more about Perceptual Control Theory. I love to talk about PCT. And, more importantly, PCT can help you deal with frustration, happiness, friends, parents, partners, and associates more effectively. I think it will be especially beneficial in your world travels because PCT is an explanation that applies to all living things. It crosses cultural, ethnic, gender, and economic boundaries. As you learn more about PCT you begin to realize it is all about you! Think about yourself as your own body of research to test out ideas. You can be your own walking laboratory, and every experience you have can be thought of as a new set of data to process.

This idea, that it is all about you, is the first thing I want to talk with you about. A core principle of PCT is that we control ourselves, and that's what living is all about: *controlling.* We do not have the ability to control *for* another person. Ultimately we cannot control others, which is good news and bad news all rolled into one. The good news is this releases us from trying to control others or letting them control us. The bad news is we can't control others, though many people are paid to try to do just that, such as teachers, bosses, and police officers. In some ways these professions are expected to get others to do things that they may or may not want to do. This usually develops into coercion, which is stressful for everyone. When people talk about controlling others, what they are actually doing is tapping into something another person wants. They use that information to either prevent or assist the person in getting what they want. More on that later.

You practice martial arts. A big part of your training is based on this same idea that power is within, and you know that someone else can't make you do anything, even though it may appear that way on the surface. Through earning your black belt, and in your military career being trained in security, you have learned self-discipline and are unwilling to give up your personal power by letting someone "make" you do something you don't want to. I know you have seen people lay down their lives for something in which they believe.

When I hear someone use a form of the word *make* — such as "He *made* me so angry!" or "That *makes* me sad." — I am reminded of my sons' father, who would say to me, "Shelley, would you make me a sandwich?" In my mind, I would always see a sorcerer with a magic wand saying, "Poof! You're a sandwich." The idea that someone can *make* you angry, happy, sad, jump off a bridge, learn your multiplication tables, or keep your room clean is simply not true. This idea of something outside of us *making* us feel or do something is so hard to let go of, it is one of the big shifts I hope you make while learning PCT. I think it's worth repeating... no one can make you feel or do anything without your permission.

Think about learning PCT as learning a new language and test out the ideas for yourself. Listen to yourself over the next few days and see how you use the words *make* and *made*. Where is the focus? Inside or outside? Look around you and see how often other folks attempt to *make* someone else do something, especially when it is something the other person doesn't really want to do. See if you catch yourself thinking, "That makes me ___." Watch what happens; be the observer.

Now let's get back to this idea that it's all about you. What I mean is this: everything outside of us and some stuff inside of us just "is." There is a simple PCT concept you can remember by its initials, IJI, which stands for "It's Just Information." The world is full of information. It comes in many forms, from the sounds we hear, to the things we see, to the thoughts we think, and a whole lot more. I think of this as noise — some that is music to my ears, some that is static, and some that I don't even hear — coming from the radio of life. The idea that *it is just information* can really come in handy when someone is yelling in your face, or when someone says something you aren't expecting. My guess is you have experienced this yourself.

As an American who has traveled extensively in the Middle East, there have been times when someone has been in your face loudly blaming you for U.S. foreign policy. At that moment you may have wanted to turn the radio of life to a different station or to just simply shut it off. Times like these serve as vivid reminders that no two people see "information" in exactly the same way. Times like these also serve as a reminder that it's all about you and no one can control you unless you let them. In those moments when this was happening, you may have wanted to defend the United States and you may have wanted to yell a few choice things back at the person. I also know you well enough to know that you didn't. You intuitively knew that letting the actions of someone else control you meant that you weren't being the person you wanted to be.

Take a minute and really think about this idea that we all see the information in the world differently. It seems so simple, but under stress it is difficult to remember. Have you ever asked someone what color a shirt is? Then you ask someone else and then another person and each person gives you a different answer. None of them are wrong, but they all see it and call it something different. When someone calls me and asks, "How's the weather?" and I answer, "It's gorgeous!" and then they find out that it is 40° and sunny, with 3 inches of snow melting outside, they probably think I'm crazy. But if you live in Minnesota, where I live, and it is February, this is considered a gorgeous day. On the other hand, if you live in Arizona and it is 40° in February, it certainly isn't considered gorgeous. How we take information in affects what we do. For the past four years I have traveled to Hilton Head, South Carolina, each January. I walk every day on the beach in shorts, once in a while in a bathing suit, passing people in winter jackets, hats, and gloves. These examples are a few of my personal data sets that I use to test out the idea that "it's just information." How I record that information is unique to me. It is easier to see as I sit here in a nice comfortable office, but what about when someone is in my face calling me a "filthy American." Then it isn't so easy to remember that these are just words, neutral information, noise floating around in the environment.

Maybe it will make more sense to you if you think about a joke my colleague Barnes Boffey likes to tell about baseball umpires. The gist of the story is this, the umpires get into a discussion about how they decide if a pitch is a ball or a strike. The discussion continues until one umpire speaks up and says, "Hey, it ain't nothin' till I call it!" This umpire is, of course, correct. Information, observations, noise, data isn't anything until you decide its meaning. What you pay attention to and what you do with that information happens internally. At this point I ask people to shift their awareness, to look at the same information in new and different ways.

"How you call it" is your perception and is based on the reference you are controlling for at that moment. You might think of a "reference" as the specifications for a perception.

Many people think of a reference as the desired state of something a person wants. Be careful here, because in PCT perceptions often do not involve a thought process. You work in the field of security, and you have been taught to pay attention to and record information in a specific way. You have a specific reference for safety for which you are controlling. When you walk into a building, you probably notice immediately where every exit is, where there are spots for potential snipers to hide, and a lot more about how to make the building more secure and safe for those inside. Whereas an architect or engineer will notice the structure of the building, the design flaws, and the beauty of its construction. I live near the Mall of America, the largest shopping mall in the United States, and I often go there with visitors to Minnesota. On each trip with a new person I ask them what they notice first. My engineer friends are very aware that the floors shake, my law-enforcement friends find it difficult to feel comfortable in such a large open space with so many places to hide, my shopping friends are awed by the number of stores, the kids notice the roller coaster and the rides. The same information is available to all of them, but each individual records it in her own way, based on her own references. Each of us looks at the world through our own personal lenses, so to speak. Cleaning and examining our lenses and making sure we remember "it's all about me" can be a helpful practice. As writer and filmmaker Betsy Chasse says in *What the Bleep Do We Know?*, "The only thing 'solid' in my reality is my perception of it. If I am willing to open my eyes to new possibilities, my reality can change." This is the exciting part of learning PCT — it has allowed me to open my eyes to new possibilities.

As you learn more about the theory try to open your eyes to new possibilities. You said you thought the theory sounded complicated; let me see if I can help with that. When I first start working with a group of people new to PCT I like to tell them that "the theory" is mostly about two things: the loop and the levels. The "loop" is a negative feedback loop and the levels are a nested hierarchy of loops.

It is really rather simple. Complications arise, however, when un-learning what you already know. Keep in mind that PCT has to do with the *loop* and *levels* and the ideas that *it's all about you* and *you can only control yourself.*

PCT is a theory that explains the behavior of living systems. It is both simple and complex, just like life. Someone once put it to me this way: "It's the theory that explains my own personal experience." PCT is not just about people but all living systems, including plants and animals. When I remember this, it helps me get out of the trap that what is happening involves a lot of cognition — thinking — because it doesn't. In all living systems, the system is involved in a continuous feedback process of perceiving, comparing, and action. In people, perceptions come from sensory nerves that pick up stimuli from the outside world and inside the body. Everything we experience, even within our own bodies, starts with sensory nerves sending signals into the brain and nervous system. In PCT, we say that these nerve signals get recorded as perceptions. Each living system records its own individual perceptions. (It's all about you.) I can't fire your nerve endings for you, I can't see for you, I can't touch something for you, I can't hear for you, I can't taste something for you, I can't walk for you, I can't talk for you, and I can't do your thinking. You have to do all of these things for yourself. A plant doesn't have eyes, but it still operates on the basic principles of PCT. It has a different type of sensory system. It has an exact amount of sunlight it wants (reference). It senses how much sunlight it is receiving (perception), and if it isn't enough or it is too much (comparison) it will bend (action) until it perceives it is getting just the right amount.

Just like a plant that is only aware of what it can perceive, information is just "out there" until your system perceives it. That's why a person who understands PCT thinks of behavior as the continuous process of controlling perceptions. What you perceive, what I perceive, and what the plant perceives is all going to be different. Before we get into loops and levels and this process of comparison, let me get back to my main point: It's all about you!

On paper the idea that everything outside of us "just is" may seem easy to accept, but living by this idea isn't that easy. You can test it out for yourself. Let's say I want someone to like me. From the moment I meet this person, I think, "Wow! He is perfect for me." Right now I'm standing in the hallway, and he is walking down the hall and talking with a friend. He walks past me, he doesn't look at me, and he doesn't say anything to me. It all feels like he is *doing* something to me. If I understand the theory, I know it's all about me and what I perceive at this moment "just is." It's just information, noise that I can hear as music to my heart or static or anything I want. Wait a minute here, I really like this guy, and he is ignoring me. What's wrong with me? Am I too fat? Aren't I good enough for him? Hey, why did he stop to talk to her when she's such a loser? Well, you get the idea. Here I am living in my own little world and thinking my own thoughts, and it really has nothing to do with him. It's all about me. As I said before, it's an easy concept to understand, but hard to live by!

When you wrote to me about traveling to Africa and the Balkans, you talked about what it was like to see the devastation of civil war first hand. I could imagine it because I have seen pictures, viewed movies, and read about it, but it will never carry the same impact on my system that it does on yours. When you wrote about it, you knew that anyone who hadn't been there and experienced it wouldn't completely understand. And even someone who had been there walking right beside you would have an experience different than yours. No two people could see the destruction and sense the exact same thing. In some ways, we all live in our own little worlds brought to us by our own perceptions. No two people have the same experience and no two people want exactly the same thing.

Take time to test IJI out for yourself. Think about a situation that you were involved in with other people over the past few days and ask yourself, "Did everyone involved see 'it' the same way?" If you want to take it a step further, ask yourself "What led them to see 'it' that way?" Here's a personal example: I went with a group of friends to see a variety show in a small town close to home. The host came out on stage soon after the performance began, apparently crying. He started out by saying that the cast was between the ages of 55 and 85. He then went on to talk about a cast member who had been performing yearly in the show since it began eleven years ago. I'll stop there to make my point. On the way home, a couple of us got to talking about this particular part of the show. We pretty much agreed that he appeared to be crying, and we all heard and recalled the same words. Then someone mentioned how they were waiting for the punch line, someone else in the car said, "Me, too!" I, on the other hand, thought he was going to talk about someone in the cast who had died during rehearsals. We all saw and heard the same thing. It was just information until we put our own meaning to it. The meaning we put on it had more to do with who we are, our past, and our present. For each of us it was "all about us." We have a saying in PCT circles that is a corollary to this idea: "You can't tell what someone else is doing by seeing what they are doing." Turns out none of us predicted the situation correctly; it was not a joke and no one had died. One cast member for physical reasons was unable to perform the entire show and the one dance number she was going to be in on this particular day was going to be her last performance with the group.

Before I close this letter, let's take a closer look at the meaning of the theory's name: Perceptual Control Theory. When I say it to you, what do you think about? Many people think I'm going to help them learn techniques and strategies to get other folks to do what they want them to do. In other words, learn better ways to control others. Being a security officer, this might be really helpful to know. When you began to practice martial arts, you probably thought you were going to learn how to better physically control others. But soon you figured out that the practice of martial arts is really about finding ways to better control yourself, both mentally and physically. Learning martial arts is analogous to what learning PCT is all about: better self-control. The best way to set up the big picture is by taking a close look at the title of Bill Powers' original book, *Behavior: The Control of Perception*. It's not about controlling others. PCT is all about how we constantly try to control our own perceptions. Control theory is about how we act on the world to bring about the conditions we desire. For me, it's all about me. And for you, it's all about you. That's why everything "just is" until I perceive "it." Once I perceive "it," it is part of my own personal world.

I begin with this idea because it is critical to everything else I want to share with you about PCT. Although I will talk later about relationships, you must first understand and apply PCT ideas to yourself. The art and detail of carrying out PCT principles will be unique to you. Illustrator Rick Watlington, who created the cover art for this book, practices multiple martial arts. Rick put it to me this way: "Bruce Lee's Jeet Kun Do was called the art of continuing knowledge. PCT to me is a type of psychology that evolves with the person and his experiences." You're the one you have to live with for the rest of your life. The next time something isn't going the way you want, remember that "it's just information." The rest is up to you! And it is all about you!

Be careful what you perceive!

In a nutshell

🕊 PCT explains that each living system acts on the world to maintain the world that particular system wants.

🕊 Humans and other living systems do not operate based on linear stimulus and response; they are continuously involved in a process of controlling perceptions.

🕊 Nothing and no one can control us. However, others can try to understand what we want and attempt to use that information to get us to do what they want us to do.

🕊 It's all about you, how you take in the world around you, and how you control for your own unique perceptions.

🕊 Remember the concept IJI — It's Just Information.

CHAPTER 3

Dear Jodene,

Controlling is
what living
is all about

*O*ne of the individuals who inspired me to write this book as a series of letters is Jodene. When we first met at a training session, I was partnered with Jodene for a small group exercise in which participants were asked to try out some of the language of PCT. In fact it was his first opportunity to "try it on," to try asking questions in the ways we had learned about in training. Many people would have been intimidated when asked to partner with one of the instructors, but Jodene wasn't.

Besides being an art teacher in a rural middle school, he is a recovering addict and an addictions counselor. His personal and professional interest in the treatment of addictions and his never-ending quest to enhance his skills as a teacher brought him to the training. His understanding of the Twelve-Step Program for Alcoholics Anonymous played a key role in his quick grasp of the ideas he was learning in the training.

Jodene is dedicated to being the change he wants to see in the world and to living one day at a time. By modeling successful life skills for black male youths and helping individuals become more of who they want to be.

Many of our discussions have led to how PCT is different than what he already knows and does. This has not been easy to sort out. When he first asked me for my insights, I was reminded of something in Eric Jensen's work on brain compatible instruction: some learners learn by figuring out how what they are being taught is unlike what they already know. In the classroom, it may seem like these learners are challenging the teacher, but it is their way of making sense of the world. Jensen refers to this type of learner as a "mismatcher." Viewers of television shows that feature crime scene investigations are already familiar with this idea. Effective investigators look for what doesn't fit. One of my favorite TV detectives is the character Monk, played by Tony

Shalhoub. Monk is so obsessed with order that he quickly figures out what doesn't fit.

Understanding PCT has helped me see that the "mis-matchers" label might be true of all of us. We are all going about the world looking for what's not working or what doesn't fit. What is working is not the focus our attention. This ongoing dialog about how PCT is different from other models of human behavior and how PCT practices differ from other "helping" practices is the basis for this letter.

Dear Jodene,

I know you are the kind of person who likes practical, real life examples, and you don't like to be buried in all that *technical lingo*, so I'll do my best to keep it practical. I also know that you are really trying to understand how Perceptual Control Theory fits or doesn't fit with what you know. One thing I keep hearing you struggle with is the understanding that PCT is not a program or something we do. This is a very common problem when people first learn about PCT. They'll say things like "I tried *it*, and *it* didn't work," or "I wish I was more fluent in doing *it*!" What I hear you doing is comparing *it* to other programs you know and understand. PCT is an explanation of human behavior. It isn't something you do, and it is not another program. Like other scientific theories, it attempts to help you better understand what is happening in the world. I'm hoping that learning more about PCT will help you to be more effective and more efficient in everyday life. PCT can also help explain why certain programs, like the Twelve-Step Program and peer mediation programs have a good chance of being successful, but don't always work. Just keep in mind that PCT is not a program, it's a theory.

I'll see if I can find an example from the art world. I'll also try to keep my explanation relevant. I'm asking you to change your paradigm of human behavior, which will be much easier if I use examples that are familiar to you. You asked me to help you understand what I meant by *controlling*, and what makes it such a big deal. Well, let me address the last part first.

What's the big deal about controlling? The big deal, simply put, is that *controlling* is what distinguishes living things from non-living things. Controlling is required to keep people, plants, and animals alive. You see, controlling is a phenomenon that only living systems do. It is a process of reducing error in the system. Non-living things like rocks, sand, paint, or water respond to external stimuli, which means that they operate based on events outside of themselves. They act consistently, according to basic principles, with predictable results. You can use physics and linear thinking to describe the basic principles by which non-living things respond to their environments. Let me give you an example: if I mix the exact same proportions of a specific pigment to paint base, I will always get the same color. Rocks, paint, sand, and water are predictable. Living things, on the other hand, are not predictable. Living systems are able to create identical results by varying means or varying results with the same means. When is the last time you met a totally predictable person? This seems like common sense. Living systems are not predictable, but how many people live by this understanding?

Living things are flexible, not static. Non-living things can be controlled from the outside. They can be pushed, shoved, and manipulated in the same manner time after time with the same results. And they operate based on stimulus-response. You may think, well that's true of people, too. You may think they can be pushed, shoved, and manipulated. The difference is that you cannot predict what will happen when a living system is the "thing" being stimulated. When we are talking about exerting external force on non-living things, we are evoking the laws of physics. Acceleration is inversely proportional to the mass of the object. If I kick a ball with my foot, the ball moves. How far and how fast and in what direction can be predicted using the laws of physics and conditions in the environment at that moment. On the other hand, because you are a living system, if I kick you, I'm not sure what will happen. That's because you are controlling, not being controlled. With a living system I can never be sure that if I do "this," I'll get "that." I don't know that if I pet the dog, the dog will lick my hand. Even though for the past three years every time I've petted the dog, the dog has licked me, today may be the day the dog won't.

The big deal is this: living systems control, they are not controlled by either internal or external forces. As living systems, we just "do it." We control. There is no direct link from something inside of us or outside of us that makes us do what we do. This is why learning strategies and applying specific programs doesn't necessarily work. No one can guarantee that they can get a living system to do something they want it to do all of the time. There is a very old joke that illustrates this: "How many psychiatrists does it take to change a light bulb?" The answer: "One, but the light bulb has to want to change." That's one of the major differences between living and non-living things: living systems have to want to!

Most people believe that we do what we do to meet a need, and if you understand this you can control people and animals through the effective use of punishments and rewards. Provide what they want to get them to repeat an action, or deny what they want to get them to stop an action. The belief is that people and animals are being controlled from the outside, and something in the environment or some internal need is "making" them do what they do. Both of these ideas represent a linear stimulus-response way of thinking about behavior. Take a minute and think about how often this paradigm of external control bubbles up into how you think and act.

Unlike the stimulus-response explanation of behavior, PCT is not linear. It is circular, and it is about relationships.

Specifically, controlling is about the relationship between a perception (a have) and a reference (a want to have). Both pieces of information are vital, but knowing them is not enough. You also need to understand how they are related. You can't just look at a reference, what a person wants, or a perception, what they think they are getting. You have to look at both and understand the relationship between the two. Is the "getting" enough, too much, or too little compared with the "wanting."

That brings up another issue: "What are we doing?" A lot of folks think of behavior as the "actions" we observe, but that isn't what I mean by the word *behavior*. This idea of our observable actions being equivalent to behavior is archaic. Actions are only what I can see of you and you can see of me, and most of what I think of as behavior is happening inside a person and is not observable to the naked eye. Behavior is a process. To add to the confusion, we don't always do the same thing (take the same action) to get the same results. I don't always wave when I want to get someone's attention. Sometimes I whistle, sometimes I send flowers, sometimes I raise my hand, sometimes I write a letter, sometimes I instant message, sometimes I toot my car horn, and sometimes I say hello. Sometimes when I do these things, I'm not trying to get anyone's attention. For example, today a six-month-old baby was at my house, and she began to use her muscles to stiffen her body and cry. There were three adults present, and none of us could figure out what she wanted. We could clearly see the actions she was taking. We could observe what is commonly called her "behavior," but it gave us very few clues about what she was doing or how to help her. The situation illustrates the fact that neither you nor I nor anyone else can tell what someone is doing by watching what they are doing. Even when it comes to my own actions, I am not always fully aware of what I'm doing and what it's all about. I often catch myself about to pop a piece of chocolate candy in my mouth and wonder, "What am I doing?" PCT is different because it takes into account the unpredictability and variety of living in an ever-changing world, and it describes behavior as a circular process of feedback, not simply the observable actions of a person. The big deal about controlling is that it is the process that defines living systems.

Now for the more technically difficult question: What does a person who uses PCT lingo mean when they say "controlling"? Let me use an example that everyone has experienced. From the moment you were alive you were controlling for things like a full stomach, a dry bottom, a feeling of security, and other "wants." When you were young, you depended a great deal on the actions of someone else to provide you with what you wanted, and you were also constantly engaged in a process of controlling. When you felt life wasn't the way you wanted it to be, you did what you could — cry, giggle, kick, scream, and cry some more — to try to get what you wanted. It didn't matter to you that your parents were trying to take a shower, get some sleep, or talk on the phone. Your world was all about you, just like their world was all about them. For you, it was and is about you getting your perceptions of the world to match the world you want. You knew how you wanted your bottom to feel, and you knew when it didn't feel that way. It was all about you getting that "just right" feeling. Controlling is the process by which living systems match a perception and a reference perception. It's about reducing the difference between the world I'm experiencing and the way I want the world to be.

Let's get back to the example of you as a baby. It may appear that you were controlling your parents by crying, kicking, and screaming, but you were not. There were times when you took action and no one changed you, fed you, or picked you up. This happened for several reasons. Those around you had to make their best guess as to what you were controlling for, what you wanted, and sometimes they were right, and sometimes they were wrong. And at the same time your parents were also controlling; for your parents it was about them getting their perceptions to match what they wanted. Luckily for you, that included feeding you, changing you, and picking you up, or just about anything to get you to stop crying.

We have all seen parents who do not want to help create the world their children want. They are busy creating the world they want, which may or may not include providing for their children. All parents have a reference for the kind of parent they want to be. Luckily for babies around the world, most people want to be the type of parent that provides for her children. What you need to remember is that it's all about everyone controlling for the world he wants. No two of us want the same thing, and no two of us go about getting it in exactly the same way. In fact, we usually don't go about getting the world we want in the same way twice.

The simple technical answer is this: control is about a living system reducing error by taking action to try to match a reference signal and a perceptual signal. Metaphorically we are always asking: Is P (perception) = to R (reference)? Take for instance a young child in a grocery store who wants a piece of candy. What action does she take to control for the piece of candy? What does she try? She may cry, whine, kick, scream, and cry some more, acting out in what most of us call a temper tantrum. For the child in the grocery store, the reference signal is "candy" and the perceptual signal at that moment is "zero" (what you think of as "no candy"). So the child, living system that she is, continues to control for the candy, because P does not equal R. In this case, the child may use crying, screaming, grabbing for some candy, or throwing something within reach to get that candy.

Let's say the parent hands the child a pack of gum. How does that change things? The child is now probably recording a perception other than "zero." So the question is, does P now equal R? Does the child have a "match"? We don't know. It depends on whether or not a pack of gum matches the child's reference for "candy." If it does match, the child probably stops controlling for the candy. If it doesn't match, the child probably keeps controlling for candy. The child may do this by crying louder, screaming more, or adding a few other creative techniques to get what she wants. Like the child wanting candy, we are all going about trying to get a match between our perceptions (haves) and our references (wants).

Remember that I once told you PCT can be simple, and then it gets complex really fast? Well, this is what I was talking about. It is tough enough when we are working with one control system, but in this example we have two: the parent and the child. Typically, the child wants the candy, and the adult wants the child to be quiet. So what do we see? If I'm thinking inside the stimulus-response box, I might see a power struggle in which the adult thinks, "I have to win! I need to punish or reward my child's actions so that she no longer behaves this way in public." What do I see if I'm thinking outside the stimulus-response box? If I'm thinking in terms of PCT, I see two living systems both controlling to get the world to match their personal specifications. I usually ask the child, "How's it working?" At this point many children stop, because they understand that what they are doing isn't getting them what they want. At this point most parents are stymied and silent. I'm never sure if this is because a perfect stranger butted into the situation or because the child is quiet. This simple idea of understanding that people are always controlling can be extremely helpful in taking more effective control of my own life.

If PCT explains all living systems, what's the difference between controlling in adults and babies? Not much! We adults seem to think we are different than children, but we are still all about controlling to get the world to be the way we want it to be — we adults just have a lot more we are controlling for. Adults have more wants. Think about it. Have you ever seen adults who aren't getting what they want? Do their actions look much different from those of a baby or a toddler or a teenager? As adults, we want a lot more, and many people become more creative about getting what they want as they age, but it is still the same process. Check it out for yourself. Watch people around you, and see what they try. Recently on a trip home from South Carolina, I was in a very small plane late at night. I don't think there were any empty seats. It was one of those planes that seats two people on each side. The man across the aisle was getting more and more agitated the longer we sat waiting to take off. He began to mumble under his breath. I won't say what he said as it wasn't very polite. Pretty soon he was complaining about everything the airline hostess said and did, even when she was making announcements that FAA regulations require her to make prior to take off. The longer it took us to get up in the air, the more he complained, swore and moved around in his seat, throwing his arms in the air and stomping his feet. I was very tempted to lean over and say, "How's it working for you?" or "Is what you are doing helping us to take off any faster?" Here's another example. The other day, I was sitting in McDonald's and overheard one of the workers complaining that she did not want to work the 4–11 shift, the shift she was currently working. On her break, I saw her walk across the parking lot to smoke a cigarette and call someone on her cell phone.

She then walked back in and told the manager she had to leave because her mother had just had a heart attack. Now that's creative adult behavior in action.

Besides throwing a tantrum or lying when we aren't getting what we want, many of us have other problems controlling. For example, we keep using the same actions, thinking that this time they will get us something different. I'm guilty of this as well. About twice a week, I walk into my family room, and there is a mess on the coffee table. I say, "Guys, do you think you could pick up your mess?" and my boys almost always say the same thing: "What mess?" You'd think I'd learn that saying what I'm saying doesn't get me what I want, and I'd stop doing it. After all, my sons are 21 and 16, and this line hasn't worked yet. When I'm trying to be a little more creative, I say "I see 'not me' and 'I don't know' have been here. Do you suppose they could come back and clean up this mess?"

I really think this idea of doing the same thing and expecting something different is important to mention because I've noticed that as adults, it is hard for us to stop trying the same things we tried yesterday, last week, last year, or as a child. For some of us, learning that if we keep doing what we are doing, we will probably keep getting what we are getting can take a lifetime. If I base my life in the principles of PCT, I realize that action, perception, and references are all intricate parts of the process. I can take more effective control of my life if I really start thinking and being aware of *all three* parts of the process and how they fit together. I can try to be aware of what I want in every situation, question what information I am paying attention to, and attend to the actions I am taking. It doesn't hurt every now and then to ask myself, "How is that working for me?"

Remember that learning PCT is like learning new meanings for words you already know well. "Controlling" is one of those words. Living systems are engaged in a continuous process of controlling for a match between their perceptions and their references. Controlling involves action, perception, and comparison. Each of these terms has a very precise meaning that is critical if you are really trying to understand PCT. Controlling is how living systems create the same results by doing different things. Controlling is how the soccer player can get the ball in the net time after time even though he is in a different place on the field, or there are different conditions on the field, or the player is tired or fresh just coming off the bench. It is what you did when you were a baby and you didn't like your empty stomach or your wet diaper. It is what the child who wants candy is doing, and it's what the guy stuck on the airplane and the employee at McDonalds were doing. And controlling is what I am doing right now. It is what keeps us alive. Becoming more effective at controlling is what learning PCT is all about.

Let me see if I can pull this all together for you by using a painting example, since that's how you like to express your artistic side. Let's say you have in your mind's eye an idea for a specific color you want the sky to be in a painting. Do you simply go to your tray of colors and begin to put the paint on the canvas? No, you don't. Any good artist knows that colors are a blend of several pigments. This was a problem when you were in kindergarten and the school supply list said "Crayons, box of 8 colors." You couldn't get the colors to match the way you wanted them to be. Like an infant, your options for getting what you wanted were limited. Having more options can be very important when it comes to getting what you want. I know that you work two mornings a week with a group of black male youth and that much of what you are doing with them is helping them "gain options for getting what they want." You are helping them discover words, thoughts, and actions that can get them more of what they want, and much of this you do by modeling for them. Just as when you were that budding kindergarten artist, you now want more colors to choose from. You want your colors to look "just right."

So you have a "just right" for the color of the sky you want to paint. The "just right" is called a *reference*, a specific state of a perception; in this case a visual perception. And as you begin to blend colors (this would be your action) on your palette you constantly look at the color you've created (perception), and you keep blending and adding until you get a match between the specific color you had in mind (your reference), and what you see on your palette (your perception). In other words, you *controlled* for the color you wanted. That's what the term *control* means for someone who understands PCT. It is the process of creating a closer match between the reference (the specific perception we want) and the perception (the perception we are presently recording). Mathematically speaking, you are controlling for P to equal R. Sometimes you will accept "close enough," and sometimes you want an exact match. For you as a painter, the references you have for color and the other elements of art — line, form, shape, space, texture, and value — are much more specific and probably more important to you than they are to me as a mathematician.

As long as we are talking about painting I want to briefly introduce another PCT concept — levels of perception. I'd like to invite you to think about the relationship between the principles of art (a higher level of perception) and the elements of art. Specifically that the principles of art — balance, contrast, emphasis, proportion, pattern, rhythm, unity, and variety — are created by using lower level references that you think of as the elements of art.

All this talk about the exact color you want reminds me of another concept that I want to encourage you to apply to yourself: "Seek the reference." It is important to be clear on what you want, to know in any given moment what you are controlling for. What experts in any field are good at is being very precise in the references they are controlling for. For you, it may be the color of the sky you wish to paint. For me, it may be having my checkbook balanced. This concept of being very clear on what you want — seeking the reference — is one that can change a whole lot in your life if you begin to practice it. Understand what you are controlling for by seeking the reference, and don't stop at the first thing that comes to mind. Keep digging deeper. The same holds true when you are working with others. When you are asking questions, try to find out what the person wants, and keep digging. Sometimes we have to dig deep to clarify what we really want.

So all of us are living life trying to get what we want. This process is described in PCT as *controlling*. This is where the loop comes in. It is a diagram that shows the process of control. The trick is figuring out how I get what I want in a way that doesn't hurt me or interfere with others. Now that's tough. That's a letter for another day.

I hope this helps you get more of what you want.

In a nutshell

- Perceptual Control Theory isn't something you do; it is an explanation of human behavior.

- Control is important because it is what makes living systems unique; it's what life is all about.

- Understanding controlling is critical to understanding human behavior.

- Controlling is a process by which living systems bring about the perceptions they desire.

- Controlling involves references, perceptions, and comparison.

- Controlling allows living things to take different actions to get the same results.

- Understanding PCT can help you become more effective at controlling.

- "Seeking the reference" — knowing what you want — can be helpful.

CHAPTER 4

Dear Chris,

The loop is
a diagram
of the process
of control

I am amazed that as we travel though life's journey we often do not realize the impact we have on the lives of others. There have been times in my life when a complete stranger has taken a moment to make eye contact or smile or make a brief comment in passing, and days later I find myself thinking back to those moments, realizing how that nanosecond of human contact changed my whole day, my week, or sometimes my life. When I remember these encounters, I tell myself that when I meet someone, I cannot predict how my actions may change that person's journey or my own. Meeting Chris, a school counselor, was one of these life-changing moments. Chris was a participant in one of my Midwest training sessions who has now become a friend, a confidante, and a fellow seeker.

Today Chris and I still work together, developing ways to teach Perceptual Control Theory to the students she serves, the teachers she supports, and the administrators who rely on her to carry the torch. During the years we have worked together we have had many discussions about how to integrate the teaching of PCT into her elementary counseling curriculum. This letter reflects the culmination of several of these discussions. It focuses on strategies we have developed to teach the loop, a simple version of the diagram that illustrates the process of controlling to students as young as second grade.

Teaching others tests our own understanding.

Dear Chris,

*I*t has really been fun working with you over the past months, helping you use the lessons you are teaching to the elementary students in your guidance program to help you better understand Perceptual Control Theory. When I see how your personal understanding of PCT has helped you work with students, I am reassured that understanding the theory means much more than being able to describe the loop and the levels.

You asked me to write up how I might explain a very basic loop, the diagram we use to represent the process of controlling, to a group of third and fourth graders. Know that this is a very simplified version, but it will get people's thinking headed in the right direction. That's what paradigm shifts are all about — seeing and understanding the world in a new and different way.

I think I'd start by having the students think about an automatic night light or a street light. Most kids I know either have a night light or have been around enough street lights to give them personal experience to work from. If you think they aren't familiar with these examples find something similar, or create a classroom experience to draw from. Ask them to talk with a neighbor about how the light works. How does it know when to go on and when to shut off? The basic idea is that the light has a sensor, and when the sensor records *enough* light it stays off and when it records *not enough* light it comes on. It is better yet if they get the idea that the sensor sends a signal.

Controlling is about comparing a reference signal to a perceptual signal, and metaphorically the "comparator" is asking the question: Does P=R? In the diagram R stands for reference signal, P stands for perceptual signal and the box with the C represents the idea of mathematically comparing the two. Don't panic — we are only going to use a few basic operations, like addition and subtraction. And this is for you, not the kids.

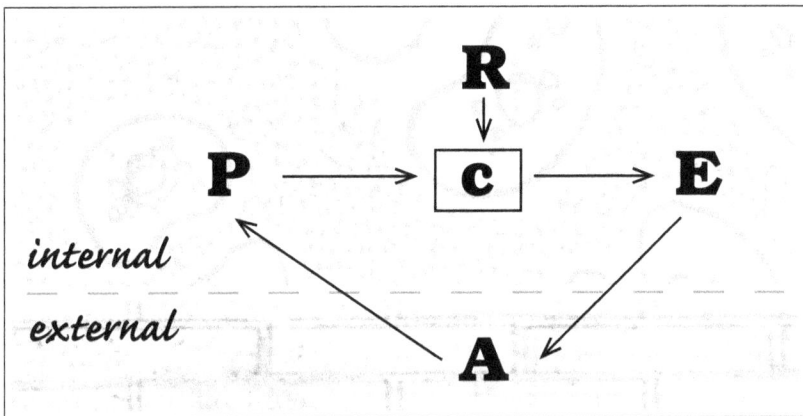

$$R \downarrow$$

P ⟶ C ⟶ E

internal

external

A

OK, so you are about half way toward understanding the loop diagram. So what does the E represent? It represents the difference between P and R at any given moment. For example if R (my reference signal) is for 10 milliliters of glucose and P (my perceptual signal) is recording 8 milliliters of glucose, then E would be 2. The difference between the reference signal and the perceptual signal — R-P=E (10-8=2) — would be not enough glucose. I need more glucose. Conversely, if R= 8 and P=10, than E would be -2, too much glucose. Subtraction is what happens mathematically in the comparator function box.

It makes a difference in the diagram if something is shown as an arrow or a box. An easy way to think about it is that boxes have a job to do — they represent a mathematical function (such as +,–, x, or ÷) — and arrows represent the transmission of neural signals. The last element we have in this simple loop is A, which stands for action. This is what I see you doing and what you see me doing. It is a lot of neural signals combining to effect muscles and glands.

Let's now think of how to explain this to the students. The night light is not a living system. It doesn't have wants (references) and perceptions the same way a human does, so what I'm doing here is anthropomorphizing, but the general idea is the same. Say that the night light has an ideal amount of light that it wants (what we call a *reference*) and the sensor in the light is constantly measuring the amount of light in the room (what we call *perception*), and only when the two don't match (what we call *error*) does the light do something (*action*). In this case, the light turns on or off by opening or closing the circuit. That's pretty much how people work: people do something when they become aware that a perception and a reference don't match.

Let's say you're watching TV and your family is busy talking about something. You have at that moment a "just right" idea of how loud you want the TV to be. In PCT, we call this a *reference*. Your brain-body system is kind of like a reference book in the library, full of information, and when you want something your brain-body "looks up" what "just right" is in that situation. In this case, you look up the reference for how loud you want the TV to be so you can hear it over your family's voices. Then, through your ears (a sensory organ) you record your *perception* of how loud the TV is right now. You *compare* these, like weighing them on a scale. Your comparator asks, "Is the TV volume too soft, too loud, or just right?" The difference between how loud you want it and how loud your ears hear it is called *error* (E). You then take *action*, you do something, to get the volume closer to "just right." The reason we show the process going around and around is that you keep trying to figure out if the TV volume is just right. The process could involve using the remote control and turning the volume up just a little, and then seeing if it is loud enough, and then maybe turning it up a little bit more, and then maybe turning it down. You get the idea.

While you're giving this explanation I would start drawing a very simple loop diagram. As a counselor, you might want to talk about what action you would take and let the kids play out some options, just to see where different actions might lead. Remember, when talking about living systems, we never really know what the result of a specific action will be. But we do have the ability to imagine, a skill that is important for students to learn. Encourage them to think about, to imagine, or to predict what might be the results of their actions.

Remind students that A, action, is all we can observe about other people. We can't tell what someone else is doing simply by looking at them, because most of what's happening is going on internally. When you ask someone what they want, you can find out what he is controlling for, what his reference is at that moment. You are trying to get to the inside of the loop. People who understand PCT ask the question *What do you want?* to let others know that we can't ever be sure what someone else is controlling for.

Teaching the loop to younger students is helpful because many of them think in pictures. It also helps build a common language around the school. After this explanation, if someone asks, What are you controlling for? What's your reference? How are you perceiving it? or What do you want? the other person is more likely to give a more meaningful answer than Huh? or I don't know.

There are a couple of things that are critical to understanding the *loop*. First: scientists refer to this type of organization as circular causation, a feedback process in which the

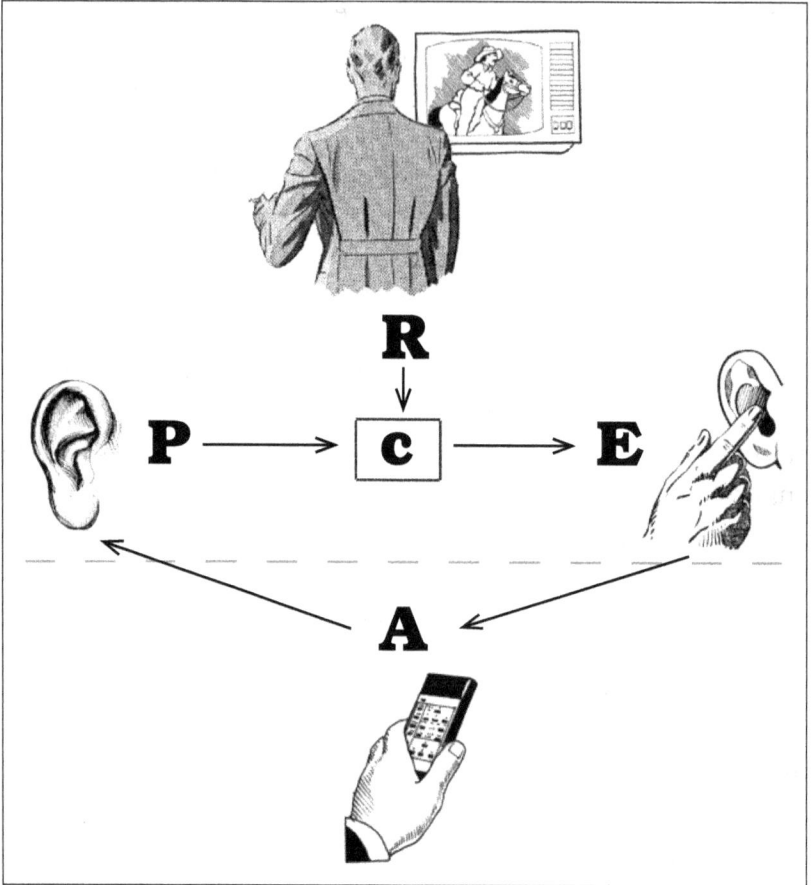

causes have consequences that affect the causes. Driving a car, steering a boat, or riding a bicycle are all great examples of this type of feedback loop. There is a children's book that I often use to illustrate this process, *The Old Ladies Who Liked Cats* by Carol Greene. In the story, one night the mayor trips over a cat and orders that cats are no longer allowed out at night. This decision creates many, many changes on the island all circling back to the cats.

Second: the PCT loop is a negative feedback loop, a specific kind of loop that is self-regulating. The feedback process is intended to move the system toward decreasing or negating error, getting a closer match between perception and reference. When I talk with adults, I like to ask them, "Do you want children to be self-regulating?" The answer is always yes. The good news is that that is how people are designed. What we need to do is learn to work with the system, not against it.

Third: Although I have described this process sequentially, it occurs simultaneously. In the nanosecond that environmental conditions change, every component of the loop changes.

Some scientists call this a self-balancing loop. Norbert Wiener, a founder of cybernetics, was aware that feedback is an important concept for modeling not only living organisms but also social systems. Sociologists have been using control theory to explain group patterns for years. Understanding the negative feedback loop is important in working with individuals and with groups.

This circular organization of cause and effect is one of the biggest differences between PCT and Stimulus-Response Theory. Feedback loops are an abstract description of patterns of relationships within an organism and throughout organizations. People are in a constant dance with their environment, trying to control their perceptions through actions on their environment, including internal actions. In the stimulus-response view, something in the environment interferes with a person, something happens inside that person, and the person acts on the environment. Three steps in a row, with a beginning and an end and the process is complete.

Stimulus-Response View

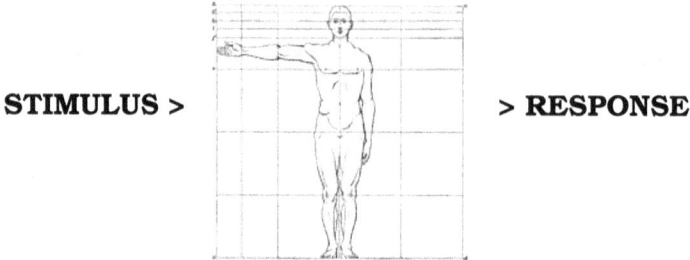

STIMULUS >   **> RESPONSE**

I don't think that is how humans work. I say something to my niece, such as, "Katie, would you please remember to put the remote control on the coffee table?" She replies, "I was sitting at the dinner room table; that's why I put it there." I assess if what Katie has said matches my references for what I wanted by saying, "Katie would you please remember to put the remote control on the coffee table?" Which, of course, it doesn't, and we have the same conversation over and over and over again. Have you ever felt like you keep having the same conversation with someone and you keep getting nowhere? That happens because you haven't matched your reference (what you want to communicate) and your perception (what you think you have communicated). This happens a lot in relationships.

We are, as living systems, constantly engaged in a circular process of trying to decrease error in our systems. We do not operate in a linear fashion. I cannot be sure that if I apply the same stimulus to the same person multiple times, I will always get the same response. All I can be sure of is that each person is trying to reduce the error in her own system.

Finally, I think it is important for you to understand that what feeds back into the loop after your action is not the action you took, but the result of the actions along with oth er environmental information. Bill Powers in *Behavior: The Control of Perception* writes: "What an organism senses affects what it does, and what it does affects what it senses."

The second time your system loops through the TV volume scenario, you don't focus on hitting the volume button twice, you are not aware of the neurons that fire to move your muscle to hit the button twice, your awareness goes to how much louder or softer the TV seems to you. Your perception may be affected by changing factors in the environment. Perhaps more people are talking, or their voices have gotten softer or louder, or perhaps a barking dog has entered the room. We've all experienced variations of this. Perhaps you were at a party, and you spoke louder in order to be heard, and all of a sudden everyone around you stopped talking, and it sounded like you were shouting. Your system took in the results of your increased volume and the other voices getting quieter, and you thought, *Oops!* (error). You couldn't predict how the environment was going to change. This is one of the difficulties in planning: the environment is not predictable and that is why we need to have variable means to get the same results. This is why we need to learn to control more effectively.

As you teach your students, just remember to draw from their own experiences. Third and fourth graders have a lot of experience with being living control systems. The more you can take their examples through this simple loop, the better chance you have for them to understand and retain the information.

Well, Chris, I hope this will help you the next time you work with the students. Let me know how it goes.

Keep on looping.

In a nutshell

- There is a dynamic relationship between any living system and its environment.

- Perceptual Control Theory is based on a process of circular causation, where there is no beginning and no end, but a continuous process of feedback.

- Circular causation has also been used to explain the causal relationships in societies, groups, and organizations.

- The diagram used to describe the process of control is a negative feedback loop, where R=reference perception, P=perception, C=comparator function, E=error, and A=action.

- We are always trying to reduce error between specific reference perceptions and our present perceptions.

- We monitor the results of our actions, not the actions themselves.

CHAPTER 5

Dear Max,

We are

a mess

of levels

It is a great pleasure to introduce you to my friend Max, a quiet soul with a big heart. I met Max during one of my training sessions, where he sat quietly pondering his inner thoughts. Participants like this often surprise me when their internal thinking leads them to ask profound questions. It was on about Day Two during the second series of four-day trainings when Max asked, "Shelley, can you help me better understand about the levels of perception? I have a feeling that understanding this will have a profound impact on my helping students in my counseling role." Of course, he was right. Understanding the levels of perception is very important when trying to help others. The basic premise of counseling is moving the client up a level: bumping it up!"

Soon after meeting Max the Counselor, I was treated to an encounter with his alter ego, Max the Musician. I was invited to a local festival, and as I was finishing a wonderful meal, in he walked, sat down, and invited me to hear his band play. Had I known during the training that he was a musician, I could have given him an explanation of the levels of perception that is the basis for this letter. This letter taps into a love for music that he, Bill Powers, and I share to examine levels of perception through the lens of musicianship.

Everything you have learned so far about the loop will come in handy. The entangling of the loops create the behavioral hierarchy known as the levels of perception.

Understanding Perceptual Control Theory can help us untangle ourselves!

Dear Max,

Let me begin by saying what fun it was to see you the other night, truly in your element, performing the music you so obviously love. I am always a bit jealous of those who continued to take their love for music to a higher level and continue to perform. At one time I played both the piano and the saxophone. I still dabble at the piano just beyond a beginner level, and after high school I stopped playing my saxophone. It now resides under my bed. I will admit it is one of the things I wish I could "do over" in my life.

When you and I were talking the other night, you asked me a lot of questions about the levels of perception. To better explain the levels, it is important that I first make sure that you have a few other basic concepts in place. Understanding Perceptual Control Theory is like constructing a building, a good fundamental foundation is critical to build the scaffold of the rest of the building. The cornerstone of PCT is that behavior is the control of perception.

Bill Powers begins with the question *Why do we need to control?* The answer is simply because the world is not exactly the way we would like it to be. If it were, we would not *behave* by controlling to create specific perceptions. You see, our world is represented to us as perceptions and we act on the world to control a match between a specific reference perception (desired state) and a perceptual signal (present state). We do not do things to meet a need or because something inside or outside of us *stimulated* us to do so. Instead, we are simply engaged in a continuous effort to

reduce error. This applies not only to what some consider our cognitive errors but also to physical errors. The bladder system is a great example. When the muscles in the bladder register something other than an ideal condition, our awareness shifts to the error and we head to the bathroom. When we were age three and the same thing occurred, we probably controlled for a higher level perception, perhaps a reference for "being a big kid" and not wanting to wet our pants.

If we cannot perceive something, it doesn't exist for us. Reference perceptions provide the specifics of how we want a given perception to be at any given moment. We set reference perceptions (sometimes called reference signals) for both our internal and external world. What fascinates me is the idea that our reference perceptions are not static, they change constantly. It might help to think of yourself as a giant reference book that is constantly being updated. One minute I want the stereo loud enough so I can hear it, and the next minute I want it quiet enough so I can concentrate on reading. Metaphorically, our perceptions serve as this massive library of the world as we know it that keeps growing and changing. It is also important to understand that the process of controlling perceptions involves three things; action, perception, and comparison. When we operate to reduce error (error being defined as the difference between a perception and a reference perception) we are controlling for a specific goal for a perception — what can be thought of as a "just right" condition.

As a musician you have a reference perception for a specific pitch, and while you're playing you are trying to "match" the pitch you have as a reference to the one you are hearing at that moment. There is an error if the pitch is too sharp or too flat. Great musicians accept very little difference between the pitch they want and the pitch they are

hearing. They also know how to act quickly and with precision to get a closer match. There's a good chance that a good musician's ability to perceive pitch may be more acute than someone else's. My brother, for example, is said to have a "great ear." He can't walk into my house without adjusting the equalizer on my stereo system. I don't recognize the differences, but he does. My guess is that you would, too.

Me, I like to sing. I have references for how I want to sound when I sing. However, I haven't learned how to control my voice very well so that I can get a match between the references inside of me and what I hear with my ears (which also happens inside of me) when I'm singing. In fact, I often say I can hear the harmony in my head, I just can't get it out of my mouth. I am better at singing on key when the person next to me sings the same part I do, or I plug one ear. When I was younger I was better yet at creating music on my saxophone. I not only had many perceptions that I could compare to reference perception with a great deal of accuracy, but I also could correct the error quickly and accurately.

Listening to my own voice is a bit tricky because there is a physical difference between hearing my voice and hearing the notes coming from an instrument I am playing. As a musician. I'm sure you've listened to yourself playing an instrument and speaking on a recording. If you are like most people, your recorded playing sounded closer to what you thought it would than your voice did. This is part of what makes behavior so complex: recording perceptions of the present state involves a whole lot of nerve bundles. When a whole lot of anything is involved, it becomes more complicated.

So now you know that we represent this process of controlling with a feedback loop. Metaphorically, we have billions of loops operating, each one representing a different

perception we have that we may be controlling to match to a specific reference perception at any given moment. All 600-plus muscles you have require two loops each. This means over 1,200 loops must operate for our muscular structure to function. If you really want to blow your mind, think about your brain containing as many neurons as there are stars in the Milky Way—about 100 billion.

Bill Powers, when talking about the levels, puts it this way: "The faint echo of the world is not inside us, but outside us. It is the world outside us that we are trying to grasp in some small partial way through building up a huge complex structure of representations inside us." These representations we call perceptions, or perceptual signals. A good place to start understanding the levels might be to think about the structure of these loops and how these loops are organized.

When you first learned to play an instrument you learned how to position your hands, how to blow or strike or strum. Because you have a degree in music education, I know you also learned to read music. What you did over time is gain the ability to perceive all of these skills. In music we often begin by learning to distinguish one pitch from another. This is how we develop a perception for the sound of middle C, for example. We gain perceptions, from the lower levels moving upward, starting with intensity through systems concepts. Once we gain the ability to perceive something, then it can be specified as a reference perception.

Once I have a perception for something, I can control for a specific state of that perception (reference perception). When your son was a baby someone probably told you that infants can only see in black, white, and shades of grey. More accurately, he could only perceive visual messages at the lowest level, intensity. He perceived the different intensities of light activating his visual sensors. Fairly quickly

he began to perceive visual images in more distinct ways, what we think of as shape, texture, color, and so on. I'm not saying he could name the colors; I'm saying he could perceive the visual images in more complex ways. Eventually, somewhere along the way, probably around the age of four, he learned names for some of the colors. With each of these changes his perceptual abilities became more complex. He was building his behavioral hierarchy, his own personal reference library of reference perceptions.

As a musician when you first began to listen to a certain style of music, like jazz, you probably had a limited repertoire of perceptions. You weren't really sure what to listen for. But now, because it is one type of music you really enjoy, you perceive and thereby have feedback loops for millions of perceptions that you are constantly comparing against specific reference perceptions as you listen to and play jazz. Although this isn't quite correct technically, I sometimes think of reference perceptions as "remembered" perceptions. We first need to be able to perceive something before we can create a reference perception, an ideal state, a "just right" for that perception at that moment in time.

I like to cook. From the first time I tasted spaghetti I began to develop perceptions for the taste of spaghetti. For a long time the type of spaghetti my mother made was the reference perception I wanted when eating spaghetti. When I began to cook, my "just right" for spaghetti changed. Now that I've tasted all sorts of spaghetti dishes, I don't have just one reference perception for spaghetti, I have many different reference perceptions. I don't always want spaghetti to taste the same. Some days, I like my sauce a bit spicier and some days a bit sweeter. Actually, eating spaghetti is a combination of many perceptions and, therefore, many reference perceptions all rolled into one. I happen to like mushrooms in my sauce. Many people don't, because they

don't like the texture, which happens to be perceived at a different level than, say, the temperature of the sauce. So I have many perceptions for spaghetti sauce and these perceptions are on different levels. The reference perception being set for each perception varies constantly. I also have a set of perceptions for how to make spaghetti sauce, which is on a different level yet. What seems simple can get complex really fast. When you are trying to understand PCT, it is best to think of an instant in time. Put your experiential DVD player on pause to gain a more detailed understanding of what's happening in that one frame.

However, life can't be lived on pause. So for most things in life — listening to jazz music, enjoying good spaghetti sauce, playing an instrument — we have multiple perceptions that we try to manifest, and these can be represented by multiple loops. All of these perceptions happen to be connected in what I affectionately think of as a giant mess, rather like a plate of spaghetti. Man, I must be hungry. This mess is developed from the time of conception until the time of death. Yes, you have perceptions and set reference perceptions before you are born. Others are developed over time through experience. Bill Powers in *Making Sense of Behavior* describes this mess of millions of reference perceptions (loops) as being organized in eleven levels: intensities, sensations, configurations, transitions, events, relationships, categories, sequences, programs, principles, and systems concepts. And in his words: "Don't take these levels I propose too seriously. A lot of people talk about them, but few have tried to do any research to see if they're real." I personally think having a basic understanding of the levels and how they relate to each other can be helpful.

You might think of yourself as millions of perceptual loops, with each loop specifying an ever-changing "just right" condition (reference perceptions). Imagine these loops

connected in a massive three-dimensional spider web. You have several perceptions for middle C. You have one that is a dot on a piece of paper in a specific place that has a relationship to some lines. Another perception is a tone, or several tones if you play different instruments. You have one perception that is a specific hand position on a keyboard, or your lips on a trumpet. You have one for the phrase "middle C." And not all of these perceptions are located on the same level. Depending on which level of perception you are operating from at any given time, middle C may be a different reference perception that you want to control for. So, as you can see, you are a mess … a mess of perceptions connected in a complex web.

I have also heard of the levels of perception compared to Chinese boxes or nested dolls that fit neatly inside one another. Though I don't think these analogies communicate the complexity or dynamism of the levels of perception, it does help convey that the levels are a nested hierarchy. You might be asking yourself what is a nested hierarchy. Hierarchies, which are used to describe how things are grouped and ordered, fall into two categories: (1) a common linear hierarchy, such as a food chain or a chain of command, or (2) a nested hierarchy such as biological taxonomy (family, genus, species) or the U.S. Army (divisions, brigades, battalions). Simply put, a *nested hierarchy* is one in which one group fits neatly and completely inside other groups. Now that you have a basic understanding of what is meant by the levels of perception being a nested hierarchy of loops, let's get back to what each of the levels are all about.

Bill Powers is also a musician, a jazz pianist who favors boogie woggie. He and I have discussed, via email, what might be some examples of the levels for music. Remember, the names of the levels are not important. What is important is understanding that our perception can be organized

into a hierarchy of increasing complexity. However, it may be helpful to explain this concept in terms of a field that you are familiar with and comfortable in. Take a few minutes and look at this musical example of the levels of perception. Think about how when you learned music your ability to control for very specific perceptions grew.

Levels of perception in musical terms*

System concept	Music
Principle	Expression, Interpretation
Program	Theme, Libretto, Symphony
Sequence	Song, Opus, Melody, Movement
Category	Name of note or song; Recitative, Choir, Instrumental sound
Relationship	Counterpoint, Harmony, Accompaniment, Contrast, Antiphony
Event	Beat, Phrase, Pause, Pizzicato, Arpeggio, Trill
Transition	Glissando, Scale, Crescendo, Diminuendo, Tempo
Configuration	Interval, Chord (sound), Signature, Clef (vision)
Sensation	Pitch, Timbre
Intensity	Loudness

*Bill Powers, October 2005

Franz Plooij, a Dutch researcher, has conducted studies on when we first acquire perceptions on each level. His work suggests that by age 75 weeks humans have perceptions at all eleven levels. Plooij's research, which was originally with chimpanzees, demonstrates that human's behavioral hierarchy is uniquely complex.

Summary of Plooij's research on newborn development*

Level	Weeks	Detail
System concept	70-75	Belief, The way things are, Sense of self, Identity
Principle	60-64	Generalizations, Criteria, Standards, Values priorities
Program	43-49	Choices, Logical procedures
Sequence	40-43	Simple or repetitive series of events and elements
Category	32-37	Words, Symbols, Chair
Relationship	22-26	Bark/dog, "Above" target, Walk "on" floor
Event	14-17	Open door, Hug, Fall, Reach
Transition	11-12	Changes in general movement
Configuration	7-9	Edges, Texture, Posture, Patterns
Sensation	Birth	Loud, Bright, Hot, How much
Intensity		Frequency of neural current

* Rijt-Plooij H.H. van de, & Plooij, Franz X. Oei, Ik Groei! (Wow, I Grow!) Utrecht-Antwerpen: Kosmos-ZK (1992). For English and other language translations, see www.livingcontrolsystems.com

When we learn, we gain perceptions from the lowest level and move up towards the higher levels. Several lower level perceptions are required to create a perception at the next level up. Another big PCT idea is that we resolve conflict by going up a level and that higher perceptual levels set goals for lower levels by sending reference signals to the lower levels.

As we learn, we gain successively more complex purposes, higher level perceptions for which we want to control. When your son was 18 months old, he already had the ability to perceive at the level of system concepts. He had some idea of how he believed the world operated and who he was in that world. Remember, being able to express in words is different than being able to perceive something. Most of us have had the experience of knowing something, but being unable to put it into words or express it to someone else. New perceptions are a lot like that. They exist within, but we cannot always express them. Remember the example of infants perceiving intensity and then color and shape, without being able to form the words for the colors or shapes. This is true for many things we learn.

Each perceptual level depends on the existence of multiple lower level perceptions. The lower you go, the more perceptions there are; the higher you go, the fewer. Also, the lower you go, the faster you perceive; the higher you go, the slower you perceive. Remember to think about these levels in terms of a complex three-dimensional web. Thinking about these levels as a two-dimensional ladder can get you off track.

When I first look at a tree I see one thing: the tree. But upon closer examination I see that a tree is made up of many branches, and each branch is made up of smaller twigs. If I take a microscope and look at a twig, I see that the twig is made up of a whole lot of smaller twig-like fibers,

and so on. The lower levels of perception are like the fibers, connected to create perceptions at the next level up. The twigs are connected to create the next level up and so on. Parts of the lower levels may serve to create more than one branch at a higher level. Before you think too linearly here, remember I said it's a mess, more like a giant 3D spider web. Always keep in mind that there is a lot more going on than meets the eye.

Let me give you an example from your own experience and existing brain research. Each neuron has between 1,000 and 10,000 synapses, or places where they connect with other neurons. These connections form networks among themselves. These integrated or connected nerve cells form something called a "neuronet." A simple way to think of these neuronets is that every one represents a thought, a memory, a skill, a piece of information, a perception. They do not stand alone; they are all interconnected. It's these interconnections that help people build complex ideas, thoughts, and skills. Take the example of an apple. The neuronets for "apple" is not one simple network of neurons. It is a much larger network that connects to other networks, such as neuronets for "red," "fruit," "round," "yummy," and so on. When you see an apple, all of these networks get involved. In the movie *First Sight*, based on a true story, a man has his sight returned to him after many years of being blind. In one scene, the doctor holds up an apple and asks, "What is this?" Until he touches it, he cannot identify it as an apple. He has not yet built a neuronet for the visual image of an apple. This is easy to understand once you know that he was blind, but there are times each day that you meet people who have no neuronets (perception) for what you are trying to explain. For example, my sons' dad and I joined the church choir — he has an excellent voice. When we first started practice he did not realize that when the notes on a

piece of sheet music go up, the pitch goes up. No one in the group thought to explain this to him, because we all read music. He had no ability to perceive the relationship of the changing position of the notes (dots on the page) to pitch.

The levels might best be drawn as millions of interconnecting loops. Similar to the *loop* being a diagram that represents the process of control. The *levels* are a way to describe the structure and relationships among the millions of perceptions we are trying to control. Understanding the levels helps us understand control of complex actions. Bill Powers explains it this way: "We can sort the world into classes of perception that show some internal order and some relationship to each other."

To keep it simple I usually think of the lower six levels as the way we take in the world. We tend to take them for granted unless we have a physical disability that interferes with our ability to perceive at these levels. There has been more research done on the lowest three levels than any of the others. I usually start discussions at the category level. After all, in the learning process we spend a great deal of time on the category level — learning the symbology and language of subjects. When I included the previous tables in this chapter, my assumption was that we already had similar references for the meanings of the words in the tables. If we don't, it is difficult to communicate. For example, when I say "chord" to you as a musician, you have a very specific reference for what I mean. If I just say "chord" to a large crowd of people, some may think I'm talking about a piece of rope or a cord of wood. Some may know I mean a musical chord but still not have a clue what that is. A lot of formalized learning in schools is about gaining new perceptions at the category level and the two just above it; sequences and programs. Ultimately, however, I hope to address a higher level perception — of how you view behav-

ior. But I cannot do this if the lower levels are not there first to build upon.

Let's take a minute to think about the next two levels, *sequence* and *program*. When you were in about second or third grade you learned a sequence in math for adding a column of two digit numbers. If I asked you to add the numbers in the problem below, how would you go about adding them?

$$
\begin{array}{r}
28 \\
32 \\
85 \\
76 \\
34 \\
25 \\
33 \\
+\ 77 \\
\hline
\end{array}
$$

The sequence or algorithm I was taught was to start in the one's column and add down: 8+2 is 10 and then 10+5 is 15 and so on. The one's column adds up to 40, so you then carrying the 4 to the top of the next column. Then repeat the process with that column. You were taught a perception at the *sequence* level for adding a bunch of two-digit numbers, a logical step-by-step procedure for solving the problem that requires you to do something in a specific order. Today you can set a reference perception for running that sequence. But you probably operated from the program level instead of following that exact sequence. A sequence looks like a list that needs to be completed in a distinct order, and a *program* looks like the network of branches on a tree in which you come to a point and have a choice which branch you're going to take ahead of time. Most of the things we *do* fall into these two levels—things like driving a car, walking, riding a bike, or playing an instrument.

My older son, Wesley, and I recently went to a local orchard. It was a warm, sunny fall day, so we decided it would be fun to try to make our way through the corn maze. We figured it wouldn't take us very long as, after all, we are both very "logical" thinkers and good with spatial relationships. We had a passel of perceptions that might be helpful. We wanted to operate at the sequence level and take it step by step. However, we were quickly faced with the fact that there were multiple paths to take, and we had to make choices at each intersection. An hour and a half later, we did manage to get out of the maze twice, but we never did find one of the hidden objects in the maze. We couldn't seem to trace our steps exactly the same way twice. While we were trying to figure out the maze, we were probably operating mostly on the program level. A lot of lower level perceptions were operating based on the program perceptions we were running. For example, walking, the intensity of light, and balance, to name a few. A few times I thought about how great it was to be with my son, which involved awareness at a higher level. But when I stepped in some mud, my focus went to my wet foot. Thinking about the levels of perception helps us understand that we have the ability to shift awareness quickly all over this hierarchy of perceptions. Bill Powers often describes this process as one of shining a flashlight in a big cathedral. We can only see a limited amount of information at any given moment.

Take a minute and think about learning to play music. Initially, you learn how to hold your hands in specific positions and then you begin to operate based on sequences like playing a scale, by moving your fingers in a precise pattern. As you become more skilled you move to the program level and later to the principles level of personal expression and interpretation. Most principles are hard to quantify. What exactly is an "accurate" interpretation of a specific piece of

music? Or "responsible" behavior? Or being "honest"? Principles are what you are trying to maintain when you carry out programs. I believe that one of the things that creates a great jam session is that everyone involved is operating on a few key principles or systems concepts, and the lower level struggle that inexperienced musicians have to hit the right note or sequence of notes isn't an issue. Boogie woggie, for example, is based on principles of a specific rhythm and pattern. Don't loose sight, however, that a great musician isn't always operating on the principles level. You still need to practice some of the lower level sequences and programs to remain skilled. The same is true for athletes, car drivers, or any other professional that requires control of higher level perceptions. Each requires a degree of meticulous control.

The metaphor of a jam session helps illustrate why I urge you to connect the references at the higher levels of perception. When you jam with other musicians, each of you is operating on similar principles, but no one knows at any given moment exactly what comes next. If you play a specific rhythm on your bass guitar, it doesn't mean the musician next to you knows exactly what they should do next. But the jam sounds good because you have connected reference perceptions at a higher level about the music you want to play. If you didn't, one of you might be playing classical, while another is playing country, and still another rock 'n' roll, which probably wouldn't sound so great. You and I can never ever have the exact same reference perception, but we can get close. When we take the time to connect references (agree on some higher level principles) we tend to be more effective together. This idea of discussing ahead of time what's important to each of us as we work together can alleviate a lot of error. If we spend time exploring our reference perceptions at the higher levels before we run into problems, we can save a lot of time and trouble down the

road. When we are both controlling for these "connected references," we have a better chance of creating beautiful music together, instead of just a bunch of noise.

In Bill Powers's seminal book published in 1973, he showed how all behavior can be understood as a hierarchy of feedback circuits—with each level working to control perceptions specified by the level above. When we "behave" we operate from the level at which we perceive and down. Think about it this way: the higher levels never tell the lower levels what to do (what specific action to take) but they set the references for the level below, and so on downward. The higher levels send a message to the lower levels to create specific conditions.

When I say to someone, "Play it so it sounds like a funeral march," I'm not telling him exactly what to do. I am asking him to match what he is playing to his reference for a funeral march, which was developed over time through experience. When I say, "Bump it up!" I want you to operate on a principles level, providing your interpretation of a funeral march. In this way I don't have to specifically tell you how fast, how slow, in what rhythm, how loud, or where to place your hands.

My musical request — for the funeral march — taps into the idea of *pull, don't push.* I can't shove my ideas into your system; I can help pull ideas out of you. Rather than telling people exactly what to do, try to create connected references at higher levels and let individuals figure out how to "make it happen" in their own way given the present conditions. How to be safe while driving, how to play jazz, how to "be respectful" to the other members of the band — these are higher level reference perceptions created by combinations of lower level perceptions. When we are able to shift awareness to a higher level of perception, we can better adjust to an ever-changing environment on the ground.

Understanding levels of perception can get a bit tricky, especially because it is sometimes called a hierarchy or behavioral hierarchy, which makes it sound like a two-dimensional system, which it's not. Just remember, don't sweat the small stuff. Understanding that we operate at multiple levels and that perceptions come first is probably enough to get you started. I heard a phrase once that helps me: *I cannot achieve what I cannot perceive.* And remember that when dealing with others, it helps to connect references at the higher levels of perception before we run into problems. The higher we go when connecting references, the less chance we have for error at the lower levels.

Don't forget, we're all a mess!

In a nutshell

🎸 Our perceptions can be thought of as a connected three-dimensional web, in what is termed a *nested hierarchy.*

🎸 Higher level loops set the references (goals) for lower levels, but do not tell them how to reach these goals.

🎸 We gain the ability to perceive starting with the lower levels and then move up.

🎸 We behave from the higher levels down. Operating from the principles level has a greater, more long-term impact on the system.

🎸 The higher levels are slower than the lower levels.

🎸 Perception comes first; I cannot achieve what I cannot perceive.

🎸 Connected references help people operate more smoothly together.

🎸 Asking questions is a great way to *pull, not push.*

CHAPTER 6

Dear Billy,

So who do you want to be when "dis" happens?

The father of my sons is a police officer. When we were first married, we lived in a very small town in Kansas where he served as the assistant chief of police. Although it was a small town, he worked homicides, narcotics, prostitution, and just about every other type of crime there is. Over our seventeen years together I saw the justice system up close and personal. I saw the system from the role of being married to a law-enforcement officer, and I had people knocking on my door at all hours of the night because they knew my home would be a safe place. I visited the jail when he was the jailer, and I was the teacher of students who were sometimes the ones being arrested. Most recently I had the opportunity to teach a forty-hour life skills course* to women in the Mecklenburg County Jail in Charlotte, North Carolina. From these experiences I could understand why many students in my class reflected on the similarities between the jail and the school. In both settings, I kept thinking, "There needs to be a better way." If the system was working, we would expect to have fewer incarcerations and more students succeeding. But that isn't the case.

I have found that many people in institutions feel "dis"connected and when they learn the skills to reconnect and stay connected, they can be rich contributors to the community. My colleague Billy has been doing just that for years with people in the county jail system. Over the past twelve years, Billy and I have become not only collaborators, but also good friends.

---

* "Becoming the Woman You Really Want to Be" was originally developed by Glenn Smith in the mid-1990s. In 2001, I helped make major revisions to the curriculum, which now includes programs for men, women, and first-time juvenile offenders.

We share a passion for fundamentally changing institutional systems from the inside, one person at a time. We both are fascinated by people, their thinking, their beliefs, and their actions. We love to have long deep conversations about the biggies: politics, life, religion, spirituality, and the universe.

Or perhaps what has kept us connected over the years is our love of learning, our enthusiasm for what we do, and a shared sense of humor. This letter to Billy is a collection of many conversations we've had about changing institutions, one person at a time, and especially about helping others stay connected.

Dear Billy,

Thanks for discussing the finer points of Perceptual Control Theory with me over the weekend. It has been an interesting adventure, and every time you ask me questions, it helps me clarify my own understanding. We both know that when we teach someone else, we gain a deeper understanding of the subject. When I teach, I find out what I know and what I don't know, just as when you turn around to teach others, it becomes clear to you what questions you still have. Maybe that's why we teach, because we love to learn.

On our road trip we were discussing *disturbance.* You were telling me how the guys in jail, where you teach your life skills course, really like asking, "When 'dis' happens again, what are you going to do?" It is a great question to ask when trying to take more effective control of your life. Besides reminding us of disturbance (a PCT term) and tapping into the slang term for "disrespect," the phrase "when 'dis' happens" is also a good reminder that what is out there is nothing more than information — IJI, It's Just Information. It ain't nothin' 'til we call it.

The nature of the highly restrictive environment that the inmates are in might be part of the reason why they relate so well to "*dis*" happening. Every minute of every day someone else is trying to control them from the outside. Their world is full of disturbances, very few of which are facilitating forces that help them get what they want. The internal strength they gain from understanding that virtually no one can control another person appears to empower them to take more effective control of themselves. Jail is about one person (the jailer) trying to control someone else (the inmate). It is amazing that in such a coercive environment, individuals are really beginning to understand what "control" in PCT terms is about. It seems counter-intuitive.

Before I get much further into this idea of disturbance and maintaining self-control, I think it might help to take a few minutes to look at coercion. I've been discussing with Bill Powers, the theorist behind PCT, the idea that no one can control me. Powers wrote a post to an online discussion group: "If you have superior physical force at your disposal and set no limits on what you are willing to do to other people to make them behave as you wish, you can control them all you like." He went on to give an example of Gandhi prevailing because the consciences of the British soldiers sickened at slaughtering unresisting individuals. He closed by saying, "There is no natural law saying that one person cannot control the behavior of another." He and I debated this last statement via e-mail. My position was that I understand that you could not control *for* me ... only I can do that for my own system. You cannot perceive for me, and you can't act for me, nor can you compare for me, which are the processes involved in controlling. I asked Powers, "Isn't it really up to me? I may not be able to physically stop you from moving me from one spot to another, but if in that moment I am controlling for nonviolence, are you really controlling me when I remain calm?" My thought was that Gandhi was controlling for nonviolence, and he was getting what he wanted and not being controlled from the outside. The soldiers were controlling for not slaughtering unarmed civilians. Through all of this back and forth discussion, we came to this: *coercion* is the control of someone else's actions by force or threat. Coercion can only succeed by threatening a controlled variable from a higher level. Only when a higher level controlled variable is threatened will I take the action the coercer wants. The good thing is that most people in this world have a conscience and higher level references that keep them from committing what most people would see as horrific acts to control others. But we know that coercion happens all the time. We must ask ourselves, "What type of a world do I want to help create?" One in which people go about trying to coerce others or one where individuals learn to control themselves without interfering with others?

Let me give a simple example. I'm a mother of two sons. My sons and I are walking down the street when a big burly man walks up to me and asks for my purse. The man is trying to control my actions by threatening me with his physical size. I stand firm and do not move, and he then grabs one of my children. In all likelihood I will give him my purse in order to protect my children. When he tries to control me at a lower level (my purse, a possession) it doesn't work. But when he threatens me at a higher level (my children, precious human beings), my awareness shifts to my desire to protect my children, and I act in the way he wanted me to act and give him my purse. In reality, what I did was control for protecting my children. If threatening the children doesn't work, he may try to find a higher-level reference perception to interfere with.

There are several problems that arise when we use coercion. One is that the threats and physical force usually have to go up the levels higher and higher or become more and more extreme in order to continue working. First we use nasty words, then we grab someone, then we beat him up, then we threaten him with a gun ... you get the idea. In my humble opinion, most of this could be avoided if we would better understand and recognize disturbances that tend to arise in coercive environments. So let me get back to talking about that.

One of the things that really struck me when I came to visit the inmates you work with was that the jail environment is built on coercion. Is it any wonder why people who spend a lot of time in jail end up coercing others? It is sometimes the only model for dealing with frustration they have seen. We sometimes forget that we build our repertoire of perceptions from our experiences. We learn what we experience. This doesn't mean we can't gain new and different perceptions — that's what the life skills class is all about — but under stress we have a tendency to act in "old" ways, repeating patterns from our past.

In the jail, I found it fascinating to watch the inmates and officers interact with each other; what each group believed about behavior was very evident. The inmates you work with really understand that what's out there is just information. They know that for all intents and purposes, no one can make you do anything. Because they understand this, the inmates were more self-regulating, more self-disciplined than many of the officers who were attempting to control them using coercion.

I remember when I needed to go to the restroom and we couldn't leave anyone in the room unattended, so the last inmate left in the room attempted to walk down the hall with us. The officers immediately started questioning him, even though he was clearly with us, under your direct supervision, and he kept his head down and said nothing. The inmate was very self-disciplined and the more he kept calm and in control of himself, the more agitated the officers became. Although the officers were disturbance to him, he really thought through who he wanted to be when "*dis*" happens. What I mean by "in control of himself" is that he was operating from a higher level reference and being who he wanted to be, no matter what was happening in the environment, without hurting himself and others. When we asked him about it later, he told us that he knew the minute he saw the officers, they were going to stop him and start "getting in his face," so before we got to them he had asked himself, who do I want to be when "*dis*" happens?

So how do we promote and explain the idea that you can decide who you want to be when "*dis*" happens? How can we educate people when we don't have a life skills course to teach them? How do we best describe the meaning of disturbance as it is used in PCT? How do we help people focus on their higher level principles when they experience disturbance?

I think the easiest way to explain it might be to go back to one of the first things we teach, a simple version of the loop, and expand upon it. The loop is a diagram that shows the flow of signals during the process of controlling. The basic process of controlling our perceptions is about comparing a reference signal to a perceptual signal. By setting references for lower level loops we attempt to get a closer match between the two. As living systems, we are input systems, always attempting to control our incoming perceptions. We might think of this incoming information as partly resulting from our actions.

Take a few minutes and look at this more complex loop. What's new? What's the same? What do you think it means that some components are in boxes? What do arrows between components tell us about their relationship to each other? Why is D, *disturbance*, shown below the line?

R

P ⟶ **C** ⟶ **E**

CV ← **A**

D

P = *Perceptual Signal*
E = *Error Signal*
R = *Reference Signal*
CV = *Controlled Variable*
C = *Comparator Function*
A = *Action*
D = **Disturbance**

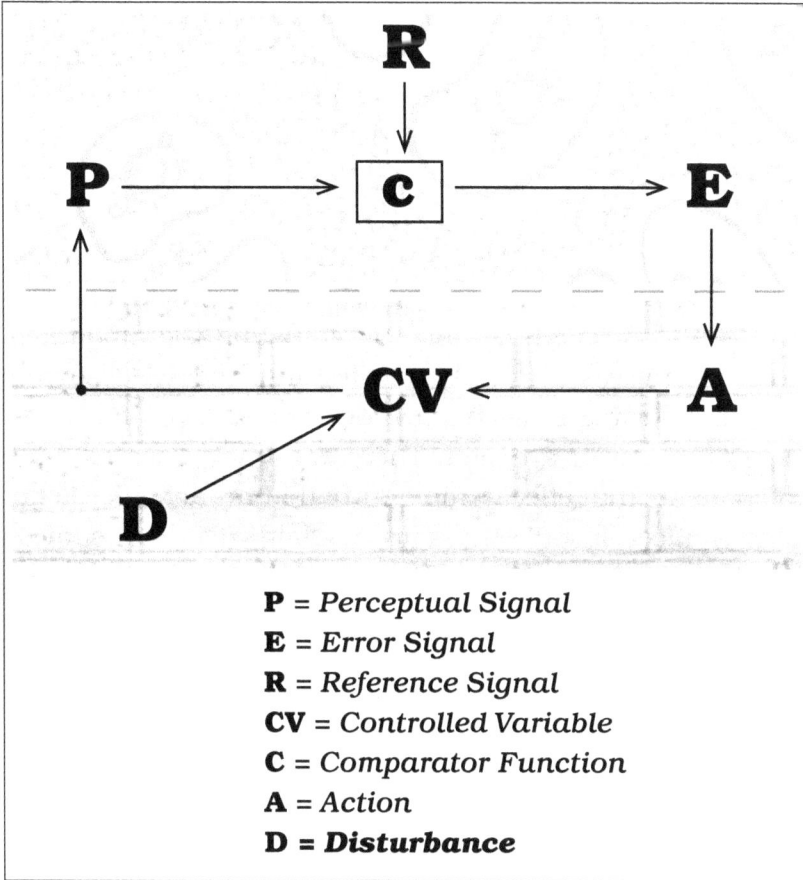

In order to understand disturbance a person first needs to understand the process and purpose of controlling. The purpose of control is to create the environment we want and desire. Think of the external environment (what is shown below the dotted line) as consisting of a whole lot of variables (things) some of which we can assert control over and some of which we cannot. *Variable* here has pretty much the same meaning as it does in math or science; it is a generic label that does not have a fixed meaning. It is used here to describe all the different factors in the environment. Inside my house, one of the environmental variables over which I have some control is the temperature. What are some others? Take a minute and create a mental list. It might be fun to compare notes with a friend. Are there some variables you cannot control?

For now let's use temperature to explain the loop. To create the "perfect" temperature for me, I have a number of options (actions I can take). I can try to control my temperature (controlled variable) by adjusting the amount of clothing I'm wearing, or by moving into the shade or the sun, or by using a mechanical device such as a fan or an air conditioner or a heater. There are other environmental components that effect temperature that my actions will not directly affect, like the humidity or cloud cover. The same is true for all living systems. Their worlds consists of a great number of variables over which they have no control and some of which they can control. Think about a sunflower: it can't control the sun or the clouds, but it can take actions that will affect the amount of light it receives. It does this by changing the direction it faces throughout the day. Play with this in your mind for a minute. Think about different living systems, both plants and animals. Ask yourself which environmental variables they can control and which they can't. The point is this: we use actions to try to create our own individual perfect worlds brought to us by our perceptions; this is why we control.

In jail, variables that inmates are able to control are more limited than in the outside world. Perhaps this is why they understand the concept more quickly; they hang on tightly to what they can control. All of us would like to be able to create the world we want; that's why we usually grab any chance we have to do just that. Every moment of every day the inmates are faced with a limited number of controllable variables, much like children in school. The adults in a school environment limit the controllable variables, often stating that they are doing this for the children's own good or the good of others. Then they wonder why kids are not more self-regulating. Learning self-control can take time, and learning to do it without harming oneself and others is important. The idea of limiting controllable variables might be one reason why so many kids today compare school to a prison. We've now circled back to the idea of a coercive environment, and one of the problems in this type of an environment is that most people want to cling tightly to what they can control. We all want more degrees of freedom to create our own ideal world. But more on that later.

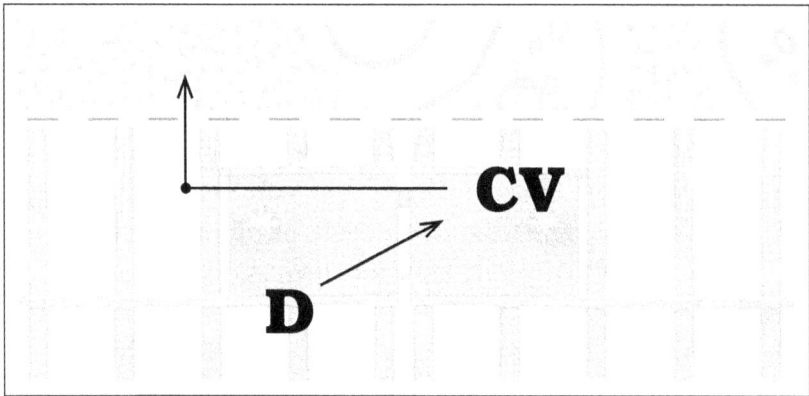

If you look at the more complex loop diagram, you may have noticed that D, *disturbance*, points to CV, the *controlled variable*. That tells you that there is a relationship between the two. To really understand disturbance you need to understand what is meant by the controlled variable. Now that can be tricky, but I've already given you a good start. Do you remember when we asked our PCT colleagues to give us an easy example to teach the idea of the controlled variable? We ended up having a two-hour discussion to try to find something everyone could agree on. Now that was an experience I'll never forget. It just goes to show this isn't easy to

teach. We eventually came up with something like this: Bob wants to walk out the door. In this case, the *reference perception* (R) Bob is controlling for is *his position* of being out the door. Therefore, at any given moment, Bob's *position* to the door is the variable being controlled, CV. In the diagram, *disturbance* is shown as affecting the controlled variable, in this case Bob's position to the door. This means there is a direct relationship between disturbance and the variable Bob is trying to control. Since the controlled variable is his position in relation to being out the door, then disturbance would be anything in the environment that would interfere or assist with Bob getting out the door, such as a gust of wind, a chair in his path, or someone yelling at him to come back inside. Bill Powers put it this way:

> Ask yourself: why does any variable have to be controlled? Answer: Because it is being influenced by processes and forces in the environment that tend to make it change (disturbances), and therefore it will not automatically come to the state that we want it to be in.
>
> We have to add our own actions to all those other influences (disturbances) in just the right way to make the variable come to the state we want and stay there. [We need to find] the right way to control that specific variable. When we succeed, we say that the variable is controlled. It is then a controlled variable.

If the environment wasn't full of influences and forces (disturbances) and the world was always exactly how we wanted it to be, we would have no need for controlling. But the environment is not static, and what we are controlling for at any given moment can change. Let's take another look at Bob. Instead of controlling for getting out the door, he may be controlling for lying down. Then the variable being controlled is again Bob's position, but now rather than his position in relation to the door, it's his position in relation to the floor, or wherever Bob wants to lie down. So now the gust of wind is still disturbance, but it might be thought of as a facilitating force, one that aids Bob in controlling his position, because the gust of wind could help him lie down, rather than hinder him. In both of these examples Bob's position is the variable under control and in one case the reference perception is for "out the door." In the other case it is for "lying down." It is important to note here that the gust of wind in and of itself is neither a facilitating force nor a hindering force, it *just is*. In this case it is disturbance, because it impacts what Bob is controlling for.

In PCT terms, disturbances are forces outside the individual that must be controlled as the person acts continually to realize her intentions. This means the guys in jail are right, life is full of disturbance! Unfortunately for them, their world in jail is jam-packed full of what they see as hindering forces. What we are all doing is going about controlling the variables in the environment so that we can get a match between our reference and our perception at the time. It's all about keeping error at a minimum.

Now back to an environment that is purposefully designed for one group (or one individual) to attempt to control another, like jail. These environments are based on coercion and therefore are intentionally designed to be full of disturbances that are, for the most part, not the facilitating kind. If you keep looping around, that means these coercive environments run a greater chance of being full of people experiencing error upon error. The more error in the system, the more action will be taken to gain effective control. The officers are intentionally acting to create what the inmates will perceive as disturbance, keeping them from getting what they want, by interfering with the inmate's ability to control the variables in the environment. In common language, the officers' job is to keep the inmates from getting what they want, unless it is exactly what the officers also want. Technically, when another person interferes with your use of the environment in such a way that you are prevented from taking action to create the perception you are controlling for, the other person disturbs your controlled variable.

Say I want a drink of water, and you are standing at the drinking fountain getting a drink. At that moment you are interfering with the environment in such a way that keeps me from getting what I want. Your being at the water fountain is disturbance, in this case a hindering force. But if I'm walking down the hall, and I just finished a twenty-ounce bottle of water, and you are standing at the drinking fountain, I probably won't even notice and you definitely won't be seen by me as disturbance. Here's another way the situation could play out. I'm walking down the hall wanting a drink of water, and you're standing at the water fountain. As I approach, you step away and keep holding the knob and the water keeps flowing. You're still disturbance, but this time you're seen as a helping force, rather than a hindering one. In both cases, when disturbance was present, I might have needed to change my action to get what I wanted. There is always a chance that you will interfere with me getting what I want in some other way, like tripping me as I walk by. The way the jail is structured it would be virtually impossible for the inmates not to perceive the officers and their actions as disturbance a lot of the time. There is a phrase that I hear my sons use that reminds me of this: "He's just messing with my head." When we don't understand PCT, we attribute what is happening inside of us to people or things in the environment. In our head, we become the victims of our environment.

If a person is always trying to get what she wants (perceiving the world how she would like it to be), then to create the perceptual input she desires, she must oppose the disturbance in the environment. In other words, when the officers and their actions are seen as a hindering disturbance, the inmates will act to override the disturbance. They are not acting to keep the officers from getting what the officers want; they are acting to allow themselves to get what they want. A common problem in coercive environments is that those being coerced (the inmates) are seen by those using coercion to control (the officers) as disrespectful, bucking authority, rude, and misbehaving. In many cases their actions are not directed at the "authority figure," they are simply trying to counteract the disturbances they are experiencing. In my opinion, the biggest problem in a coercive environment is that virtually everyone, both the officers and the inmates, have limited abilities to control. Therefore, it is an environment rich with error, action, and disturbance. Bill Powers puts is this way:

> What this boils down to is simply a fact of control: if a disturbance tends to alter a controlled variable, to maintain control we must produce an action that has an equal and opposite effect on the controlled variable. Small disturbances call for small opposing actions. Large disturbances call for large opposing actions. And violent disturbances call for violent opposing actions. The only other choice is to give up controlling the variable. The prisoners are where they are because they disturbed someone else's controlled variables — and the someone else turned out to be stronger than the prisoner. This explains why

they are in jail, but it doesn't necessarily say they belong there.

In the life skills course, we help the inmates *bump it up* by controlling for higher level variables, like thinking about what kind of people they want to be. They begin to focus on higher-level references and are able to let go of taking action to overcome lower level disturbances. One of the problems in coercive environments is created when someone figuratively pulls out a machine gun to do the job of a squirt gun. The thing to remember is that people with the "gun" pointed at them are going to oppose the strength of the disturbance.

This idea of taking large opposing actions for small disturbances is something we have all experienced. I think back to when my sons were first learning to drive. They would experience a small disturbance (a gust of wind, a pot hole, driving a bit too close to the center line) and they would whip the steering wheel as far as they could in the opposite direction, overcompensating for the disturbance. This happens when we are learning a new skill, it also happens when our ability to affect the environment is limited. In your course, you are helping the inmates control at higher levels and in ways they may never have been successful before. As with teaching my sons to drive, you are helping them learn what to pay attention to, what to let go of, and how not to over-steer.

Before we leave this discussion of disturbance, I want to emphasize one thing: disturbance should not be thought of as a bad thing... it isn't always preventing us from getting what we want. In fact, sometimes it helps us. It is always out of our control, a factor in the environment that is having an impact on what we are trying to control. Probably one of the clearest examples I have been able to come up with is tail winds and head winds. If I'm the pilot of a plane and I want to arrive exactly on time at the airport, head winds and tail winds are both disturbance. They are in the environment and I don't control them, but they have an effect on what I am trying to control, my on-time arrival at the gate. They will change every factor around the PCT loop except my reference perception for on-time arrival.

When I was visiting the jail, I was really struck by one of the inmates in your class saying, "I've really learned in your class that IJI (It's Just Information) and that I can decide who I want to be when 'dis' happens." He then explained that when he started taking your class, every time an officer was in his face (what he recorded as disturbance), he was able to remember it was just information and not to act to overcome what he used to think of as "something I have to answer to." We asked him how he knew this new approach was better, and he said, "Because I ain't been in the hold once since I started this class."

Is it any wonder in an environment where the balance of control is so lopsided, where one individual or a group of individuals are hired to control others, that we have problems with individuals learning to self-regulate or to become self-disciplined? Everyone is in a constant state of taking action to overcome the disturbances in his environment.

Just as the inmates in your class have learned to *bump it up*, my sons have learned to take a broader perspective when driving. If they focus further down the road, the little disturbances that they once felt they needed to oppose are barely noticeable. We could all take a lesson from the guys in your class and learn to shift our awareness by asking, "When '*dis*' happens, who do I want to be?"

As we go about our daily activities, the world around us is jam-packed with influences, some of which aid us in getting what we want and some of which hinder our ability to get what we want. We don't know ahead of time what will be

disturbance and what won't because it all depends on what we are trying to control for at any given moment, what we want our world to be.

For instance, today I was out to lunch with my friend Linda. Her phone started ringing just as we were about to eat lunch. She looked at the caller ID and saw it was her boyfriend calling. You and I might think, "Wow! Match!" That wasn't what happened. Instead, she groaned and said, "I'm not answering because I know he is going to want to go out to lunch." I had assumed that this disturbance was a helping force. I was thinking, "She wants to be in a relationship with this guy and he wants to take her to lunch." She went on to say. "I don't want to hurt his feelings by telling him I'm already out to lunch." For her at that moment, his number on the caller ID was perceived as a hindering force. It was a good reminder to me that we cannot tell what someone is controlling for by watching what they are doing. We had a long discussion afterwards about who she wanted to be the next time disturbance happens. What can I say, once a teacher always a teacher! Life just keeps presenting opportunities for teaching and learning.

I've often wondered if we wouldn't all benefit from participating in a life skills course, but that, my friend, is a discussion for another road trip.

I hope "dis" helps!

In a nutshell

- We are at all times trying to control variables in the environment.

- We can take action to control some of these variables and some are out of our direct control.

- Living requires us to take actions to overcome the disturbances in our ever-changing environment.

- What is a disturbance in one instance may or may not be in another.

- Disturbances are facilitating and hindering forces in the environment that affect the controlled variable.

- There is a relationship between the reference perception we are controlling for and disturbance.

- Learning what to pay attention to, what to let go of, and how not to over-steer can help us take more effective control of our lives and reduce stress.

Dear Johnson,

Untangling the entangled loops

*A*s a teacher, I am constantly asking myself when to stretch the learner and when to relax a bit. Russian psychologist Lev Vygotsky talked about the zone of proximal development, a fancy term for the gap between what a person already knows and the potential learning that can occur with assistance. I hold onto this idea when I think of my job as a teacher. I believe a teacher's job is to stretch learners a bit beyond their present understanding without stretching them beyond their reach. When I think of learning with my Perceptual Control Theory hat on, I think about error and how much error is necessary for learning to occur without the learner experiencing total frustration. When I first met Johnson in a training group, he talked about his fascination with the science of what he was learning. I thought, "Great! I've found a kindred spirit, someone like myself who loves the technical side of learning and isn't satisfied until that technical understanding leads to effective application."

In preparation for the session, each participant had been asked to plan a short presentation that described their understanding and application of what they were learning. Johnson was very excited about the risk he had taken in tackling an explanation of the loop and its relationship to what he was doing with his staff. At the end of Day One, Johnson approached me in the hall and said, "I thought I had a handle on the loop, but what we learned today just blew me out of the water! I don't know if I can go ahead with my presentation." I stood there wondering if I had stretched the learner a bit beyond his learning zone. After we talked for about five minutes, I asked Johnson about the purpose of the presentation. I asked, "Would there be a way for you to show the group how your understanding has grown beyond where it was when you planned the presentation?" I could see the wheels turning, and then Johnson turned

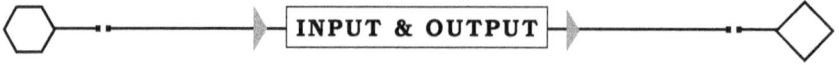

to me and said excitedly, "Are we going to get more of this tomorrow. Because if we are, I want to present first before I realize what else I don't already know."

The most important process to master in taking more effective control of your life is learning how to self-evaluate. In that moment, Johnson was demonstrating what learning PCT is all about: self-evaluation. The day after Johnson's presentation, we started talking about the levels of perception and Johnson eagerly asked, "How are the loops connected?" This question, which links an understanding of the loop to the levels, serves as the premise for this letter to Johnson.

To paraphrase Einstein: We are seeking the simplest possible answer that can tie together the observable facts. This is what I believe PCT does in helping us understand human behavior. The theory presents us with a simple explanation to a very complex process: human behavior.

Hope this stretches you just enough.

Dear Johnson,

As always, it was a pleasure to get your e-mail and find out how you, as a high school principal, are trying to model with your staff the practices aligned with Perceptual Control Theory. Your desire to understand the more technical parts of the theory is refreshing to me. When I worked with you as a trainer, you were really trying to grasp the basics of the PCT loop, and were moving towards a better understanding of the levels of perception. These concepts are the two main building blocks of PCT.

Let me start by taking a few minutes to review the basic idea of controlling, which is the beginning of understanding "the loop." The loop is a visual way of representing the process of control and helps scientists develop models to represent human behavior based on PCT. The theory is used to model human behavior with extremely high correlation rates. This process is much like what an architect friend of mine does when he builds a model to better visualize a building's design. Scientists use the PCT model to see if humans in action behave similarly to the model. Modeling is a special way of testing a theory. PCT scientists are getting excellent results with correlations in the high 90s, which means that when they are using PCT to develop models, they can virtually replicate human behavior. *

---

* See *Mind Readings: Experimental Studies of Purpose* and *More Mind Readings* by Rick Marken or the Control Systems Group website at www.perceptualcontroltheory.org/

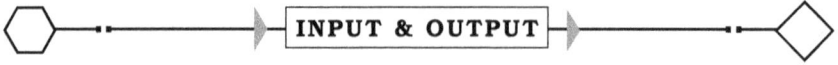

Controlling is about comparing a reference signal to a perceptual signal. Mathematically the comparator, C, subtracts R from P and determines the difference, E. You might think of this as the comparator asking, *What is the relationship of P to R? Is P too large, too small, or just right? In the diagram, C represents the idea P-R.* The answer to this equation is E, error, which represents the difference between P and R at any given moment. Thinking in math terms helps me understand the intricacies of the process. In numerical terms, an error of twelve is going to produce a lot more output than an error of two. If I'm running water for a bath, a difference of twelve will have me turning the handle much more than a difference of two. It is important to understand the significance of the size of the difference between P and R. In behavioral terms, living systems try to get as little difference between P and R, as little error, as possible. We control for our specific perceptions of the world. Teachers of PCT often refer to this as the Goldilocks Effect: too hard, too soft, just right! Like Goldilocks, we want the world to be the way we want it, "just right." The world is often not the way we want to perceive it, so we keep acting to get a closer match between our perception and our ideal references.

When you first started learning about the loop, you found out about R (references), P (perceptions), C (comparator function), E (error), and A (action). Then we added the idea of CV (controlled variable) and D (disturbance). Because you kept asking questions, you also learned that the loop has an input and an output function. If you look at the diagram, you see that input and output are shown in boxes. What does that tell you? These boxes are called *functions* rather than *signals*. These functions have a job to do, inside the box something mathematical is computed. The input function gathers incoming signals from the lower loops, the results of your action and the environment converts it into a single signal (P). The output function, O, sends the outgoing signals to the level below, by setting reference signals and what we eventually see as action at the lowest level. So how are the loops connected? To answer this, just think for a minute about what you already know: there are millions and billions of loops, these loops are organized in a nested hierarchy, and higher level loops send reference signals to lower level loops. Let this information percolate in the back of your mind as you look at the diagram.

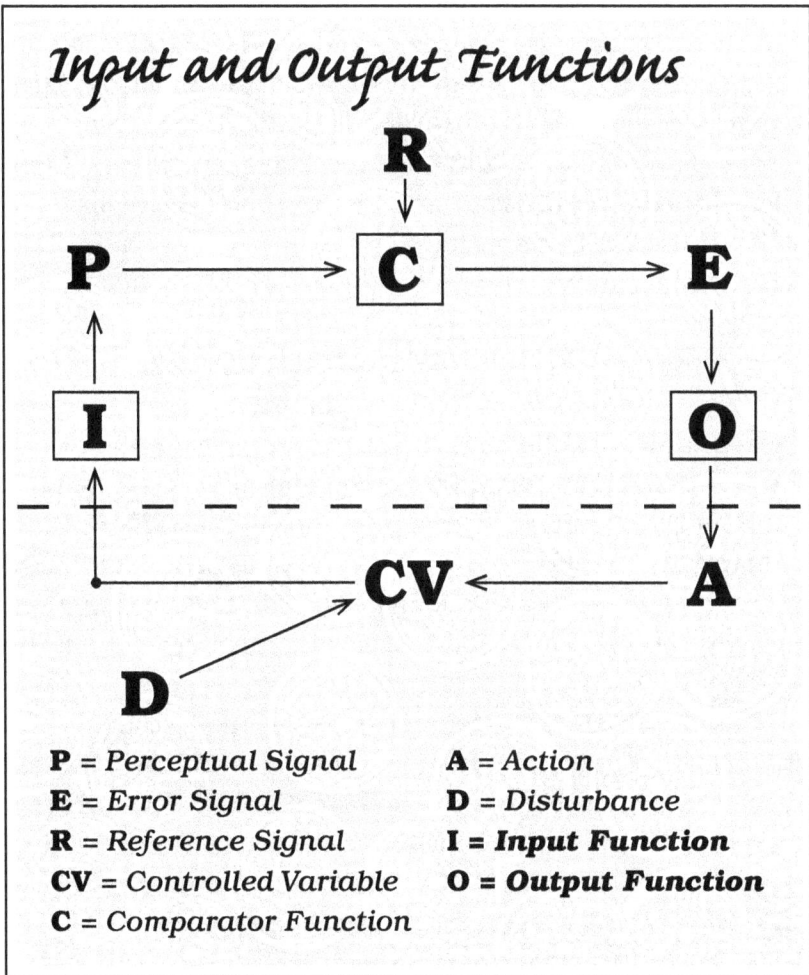

Input and Output Functions

R

P ————→ C ————→ E

I

O

— — — — — — — — — — — — — —

CV ←———— A

D

P = Perceptual Signal   A = Action
E = Error Signal   D = Disturbance
R = Reference Signal   I = **Input Function**
CV = Controlled Variable   O = **Output Function**
C = Comparator Function

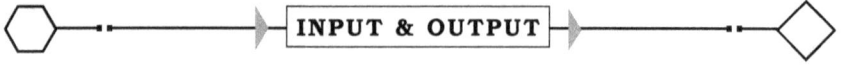

In a human, the input function is a bundle of nerve endings. The function or job of the input function (the box labeled *I*), is to convert many incoming signals into a single perceptual signal. You could think of the input function as being like a giant calculator into which you put a whole lot of information and out of which you receive a single number. This single number gets recorded as the perceptual signal. When I'm trying to explain this idea, I think about what it was like to be the scorekeeper at a basketball game. I would watch all of the action on the floor, and once in a great while I would see a ball go through the hoop. So what did I record? It depended. I could have recorded 2 points, I could have recorded 1 point, I could have recorded 3 points, or I could have recorded zero points. I had a lot of incoming information, but in the end I recorded a single number on a specific place on the score sheet. This gives you a clue about what happens on the other side of the loop.

The output function, the box labeled O, takes into account the amount of error, how important it is to control that variable, and how quickly a person wants to decrease the error. It takes all of this information and sends it to the level below in the form of reference signals. Eventually the cumulative effects of the reference signals combine to move muscles and activate glands, what we call action. Basically the output signal sets reference signals for the level below.

I know this is a bit technical, so let me use tears and crying as an example to help you understand this process. First, a little bit of background information. Dr. William Frey, a biochemist at the St. Paul-Ramsey Medical Center in Minneapolis, hypothesizes that stress — emotional or physical pressure — produces poison chemicals in the body. Different types of emotions produce different types of organic compounds such as dopamine and epinephrine in the fluid of tears. Crying removes these poisons and helps people stay healthy. Conversely, when an individual controls to suppress tears it increases stress levels and contributes to diseases aggravated by stress, such as high blood pressure, heart problems, and peptic ulcers. (Lael Wertenbaker writes about this in *Eye, Window to the World*.) Frey's research hypothesizes that we don't think "I need to cry" (choose an action) when we experience stress. We simply cry because our system, through our glands, is trying to reduce error, to get rid of poisonous chemicals. Put simply, tears release chemicals built up by stress.

You might ask how this happens. How do the glands recognize what to get rid of and what not to get rid of? They do this by setting reference perceptions (goals) for lower level loops. They don't tell the lower level loops what to do, they tell them what to control for! They basically say to the lower loops, "Create this specific condition." (This setting of goals reminds me of a line I used to love from *Star Trek*: "Mr. Crusher, make it so!") The output signal tells lower level loops to create specific conditions, a "just right" state. Metaphorically, in the tears example, the higher level loops don't say, "Secrete this much dopamine and this much epinephrine through the tear ducts." Instead, they say, "Create this balance of chemicals, and we really don't care how you do it." Bill Powers put it this way: "I'm running out of groceries (error signal) and need to shop for dinner (higher level output function). To shop for dinner I have to set reference signals for car keys in hand, wallet in pocket, shopping list in shirt pocket, door locked, key in ignition, vroom, car backing into street, and so on. Note that these are all references sent to different lower systems, telling them which perceptions to create, with no mention of the actions that bring that about."

Let's look at how we use the loop diagram to express this. Take a minute to study the figure below before reading the explanation. The perceptual signal coming from the input function is not only the result of combining several neural signals into a single perceptual signal for a particular loop, but it also acts as one piece of information feeding into the input functions going to higher level loops. Like a multi-branched tree, one branch of the perceptual signal reaches towards the comparator of that specific loop, and other branches reach towards other loops to become signals flowing into their input functions. On the other side, the output signal serves as roots reaching to the next lower level loops as reference signals.

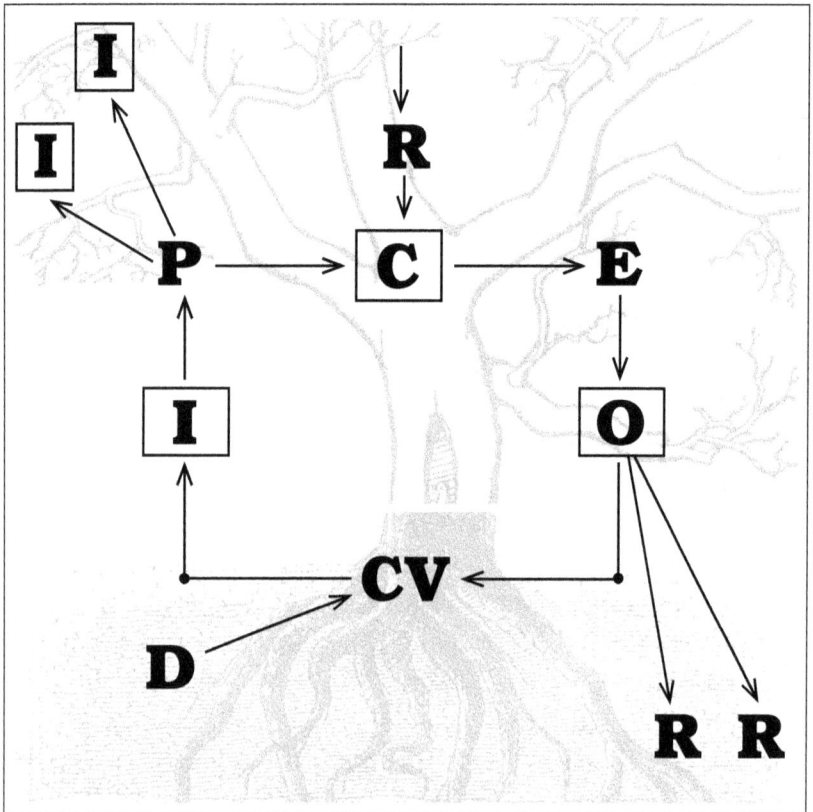

Take a few minute to think about the input and output functions before looking at the next diagram. This is a very simplified, very approximate schematic of how multiple levels of perception are connected. What do you notice?

Connecting the Levels

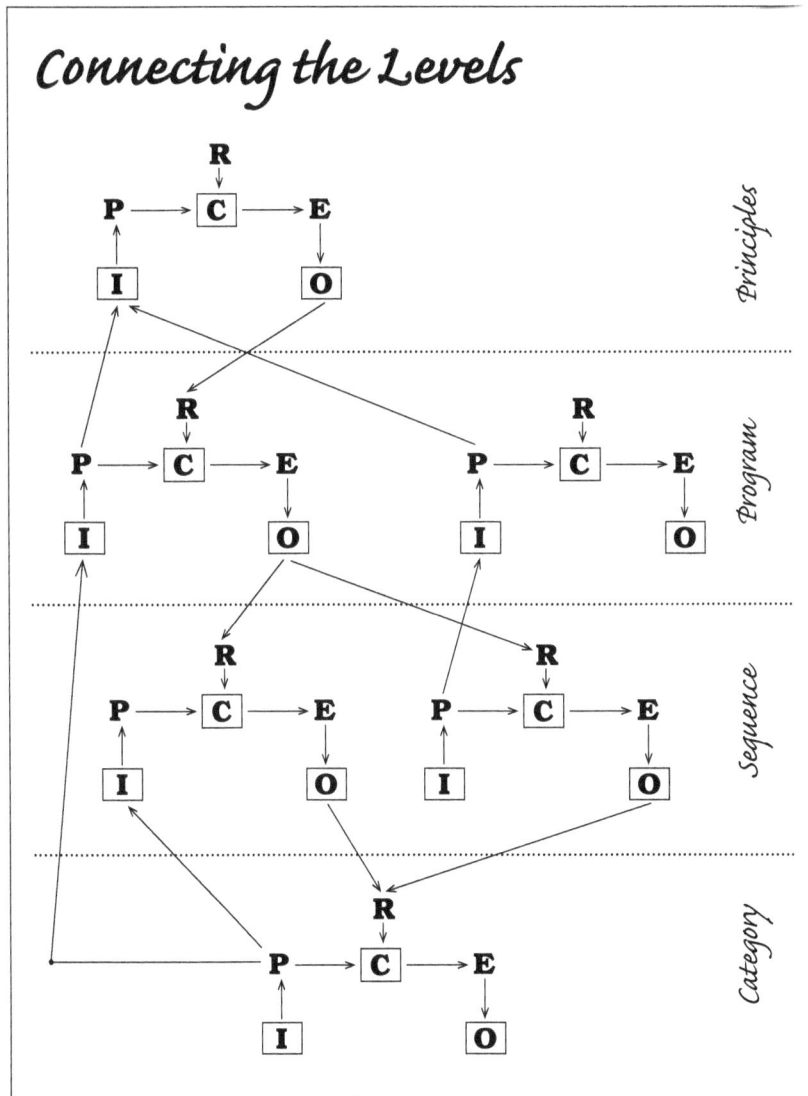

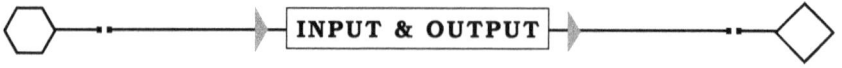

The loops are connecting like a giant three-dimensional spider web hooked together by input signals and output signals to form a hierarchy. I sometimes think of the input and output functions as flood gates on a dam, controlling the flow of the neural signals, only letting enough "water" in or out to keep the system from overflowing and to keep it running efficiently. The output signal basically duplicates itself so it can be in more than one place at a time; just as the perceptual signal basically duplicates to be in more than one place at a time.

Let's look at how we categorize the different levels of perception, and how they relate to each other using the following graphic.

Levels of Perception

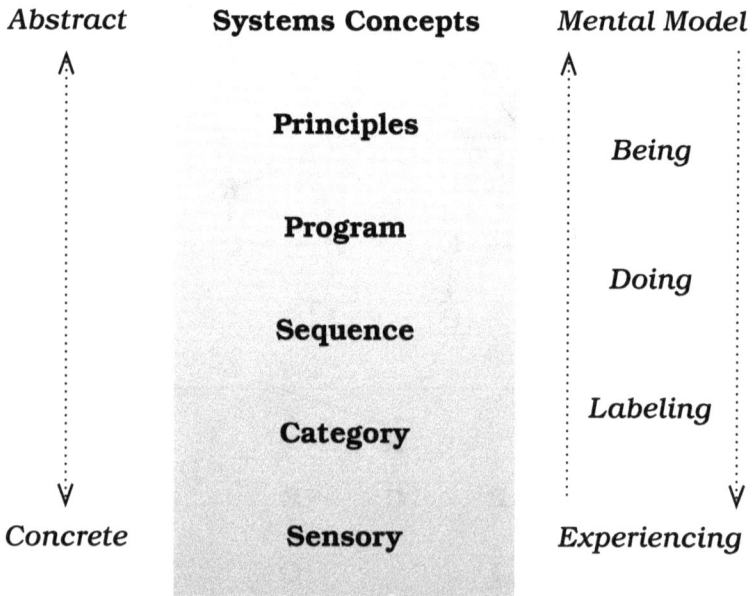

Abstract	Systems Concepts	Mental Model
↑		↑
	Principles	Being
	Program	Doing
	Sequence	
	Category	Labeling
↓		↓
Concrete	Sensory	Experiencing

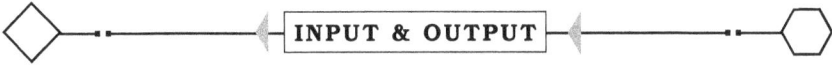

In this version I have simplified the levels. I've taken the six lower levels (intensity, sensation, configuration, transition, event and relationship) and called them *sensory*. This is the way we take in the world, shapes, size, amount, movement, etc. The next level, category, if you remember, is about labeling things, like car, chair, bicycle, square, etc. Sequence is about things in a specific order, like a scale on the piano, a mathematical algorithm, a food chain in nature, or perhaps using a recipe for the first time. Programs are like sequences, but do not need to be carried out in a specific order. Along the way we may vary the sequence depending on environmental factors. For example, a food web is more of a program level concept than a food chain. Principles are generalizations or standards. Systems concepts have to do with the way we believe the world operates.

The higher you go up the levels of perception, the more abstract things become, the slower the operation of loops, and the fewer the number of loops. The lower you go down the levels of perception, the more concrete things become, the more loops there are, and the faster they operate.

To apply these ideas to the real world, it is important to remember a couple of things. Higher level loops set references for lower level loops. This is important because if, for instance, I set a reference at the principles level, the floodgates of the output function let out a signal that eventually flows all the way down to the intensities level which is the lowest level in the sensory category. A reference that is set at a higher level will have a greater impact on the whole system, which is why I always encourage you to *bump it up*. Setting a reference at a high level leaves the details, the "how to," up to the lower level loops. As in the case of needing food and setting the reference for going to the grocery store, a whole lot of other references come into play at the lower levels.

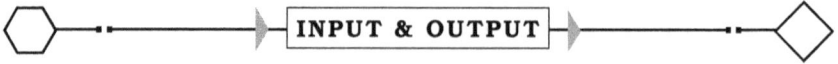

When I want significant change in a more timely fashion I can focus on a higher level reference and more things will change more rapidly. In contrast, if I focus on the lower sequence level and just try to do things in a different order, not as much change will occur. If my flashlight of awareness is shining on a higher level I illuminate a whole lot more than if it is shining on a lower level. If I point that flashlight straight down on something, I only illuminate that object. So let light shine at the higher levels to illuminate more.

The flashlight of awareness concept is also important when working with others. When we work with others for a long time, we often understand what they mean when they say "be respectful" (a higher level reference). We don't have to go into great detail with them about all the nuances of "respectful." How we came to this realization is by putting different combinations of lower level references together over time. When working with someone else, we unfortunately often use a process of trial and error, testing limits to define at lower levels what respect is. As I've seen you work with your staff and students, I know you don't tell your staff, "Stop sending students to the office." Instead, by asking them what they are hoping for when they send students to the office, you attempt to find out at the highest level possible what teachers are controlling for. You attempt to find out what principle they are trying to protect. You have learned that this works better then giving staff a laundry list of when and when not to send students to the office.

The idea of higher levels setting reference signals for lower levels helps us expedite controlling perceptions. The higher you go, the more you can accomplish with less effort. This is why I believe in operating on the principles level — then I don't have to tell you what to do in each and every situation. If I am walking down the hall and I control for a higher level reference of safety, I don't need to focus on how to walk, how

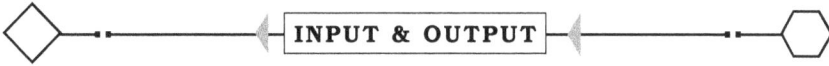

to keep my hands to myself, and how to watch out for objects in my path. I simply control for a higher level perception of safety, and the lower levels no longer draw my attention.

When I think about operating from the higher levels of perception, I find myself thinking from a more abstract and artistic perspective. As a teacher, this view helps me remember that learners must experience first, then label, then apply.

This is one of the reasons I keep asking you to draw on your own personal experiences and think about them in a new way, using the PCT model. I want you to try doing some things differently. Then, over time, you can use these PCT concepts to help you be the person you want to be in the world. You'll do this by taking lower level perceptions and rewiring them into new combinations.

So what does this have to do with interacting with others and helping those we teach? In PCT terms, we can do this most effectively by *connecting references at a higher level.* Let's take a look at one of the guiding principles that you've heard me ask you to be more aware of: *Ask, don't tell.* Setting a reference at a high level for asking questions reminds you that asking is better than telling. If you set this high level reference, then I don't need to give you a list of situations in which to "ask," and a list of what to ask in each and every situation. I couldn't possibly know in advance the details of every situation you will be in. When you know that asking questions is intended to shift awareness, and that questions that move you up the hierarchy are going to get more loops controlling with less effort, you will, over time, become more and more skilled at knowing which questions get you more of what you want.

Combining this with the idea of *pull, don't push* reminds you to ask questions in a tone that encourages self-evalua-tion and questions that are more open ended.

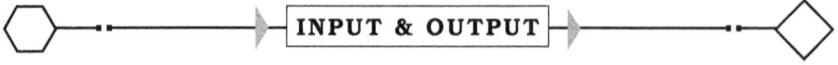

When we operate from a principles level we control for perceptions at that level rather then trying to remember a specific sequence of questions. I can't tell you exactly what words to say in a specific situation. I'm not you, and you will never encounter exactly the same experience again. Understanding PCT isn't easy, but in the long run you will become more skilled in a variety of situations if you are more aware of the levels of perception and try to operate at the principles level rather than the lower levels.

In his book *Method of Levels*, psychotherapist Tim Carey explains that asking *why* typically takes us up the hierarchy and asking *how* takes us down. So asking a teacher, "Why do you send students to the office?" and following the answer with another *why* question will generally keep moving the focus up the levels of perception. However, be aware that asking, "Why did you send *that student* to the office?" probably won't get a self-reflective answer. "Because she was being disrespectful" identifies the action of the student rather than examining the teacher's motivation. Instead of asking *why*, you might get further faster by exploring what the teacher was controlling for at the highest level. "What were you hoping for when you sent the student to the office? How would that be helpful to you?" Seeking the reference at the principles level will help you ask better questions.

Now you have several ways to keep yourself and those you work with operating at the *principles* levels:

* Ask, don't tell.
* Seek the reference.
* Pull, don't push.
* Connect references.
* Bump it up!"

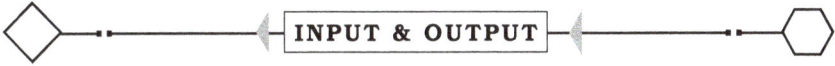

Beware that using these ideas, which are based on core behavioral principles, without understanding the theory supporting them only helps you momentarily. In order to go the long haul — to take more effective control of your life — you need to know and understand the theory. PCT isn't something you do, isn't something you turn on or off; it is a belief in the nature of how living systems operate. When it is part of how you believe the world works, it is a systems level concept.

If you are controlling for a systems level concept (the highest level) of human behavior based on PCT, then all of the principles you operate on and all of the programs you run and everything you do will be your best effort to control for a match between your understanding of PCT and the world you are creating. To keep it simple: The better you understand the theory, the more systematically you can re-fine your performance. Knowing the details of the theory allows for the artistry in the delivery.

Keep reflecting at your highest level.

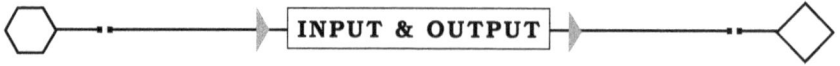

In a nutshell

- The loops are connected via the input and output functions.

- The input function combines many signals to form a single signal. We label this signal P for perception.

- The input function sends the signal (perception) to the comparator of a loop in a specific level and to the input function of higher level loops.

- The output function sends reference signals to loops on the level below.

- The output signal specifies a perception to control for (reference perception), not an action.

- The higher you operate in the hierarchy, the greater the impact on the system as a whole.

- Reference perceptions can be thought of as goals or "just right" conditions.

- Creating a systems level concept of behavior based on PCT is key to taking more effective control of your life.

CHAPTER 8

Dear Twilight,

The mystery
of awareness,
consciousness, and
the observer

I met Twilight about three years ago. Instead of trying to control my weight by focusing on food and diet, I had decided that finding an exercise routine that I would stick with and enjoy might be a healthier choice. I kept asking myself, "What would a healthy person do?" I have learned a lot about myself through this quest. I joined a local women only exercise facility, and branched out from there. I can't say I've lost a lot of weight, but I know I have less body fat, and I feel a whole lot better. It was during this exploration that I first met Twilight.

Twilight is my Pilates instructor, and over the past two and a half years we have become good friends. We share a lot of the same interests, are about the same age, and both love nature and the solace it can bring to our busy lives. We also are very interested in helping others help themselves through reflection, meditation, and self-discovery. When I began to write this book, I knew that a critical section would address the idea of consciousness, awareness, and "the observer." I realized Twilight was the person with whom I had spent the most time talking about these issues. A large part of mastering Pilates has to do with shifting awareness, being conscious of very specific perceptions and acting as the observer of oneself. For example, one night during Pilates class as I was holding my breath pondering these issues, Twilight fortunately shifted my awareness and said, "Remember to breathe," or perhaps I would have passed out and forgotten my thoughts during our sessions together. This letter is based on our discussions and emails as I have tried to help Twilight understand Perceptual Control Theory and its relationship to Pilates and exploring our "inner-space," as my son Duncan refers to it.

Keep yourself connected.

Dear Twilight,

*P*ilates class was great last night! On my way home I thought about how you always try to get us to be very precise and conscious of our movements in class, and about how you encourage us to use our minds to help create resistance in our muscles. I felt empathy for the beginner in class last night as she struggled to learn all the new positions. It is so much to pay attention to when you first start. I remember trying to get just one thing right from each exercise when I started. This is similar to ideas I try to teach about Perceptual Control Theory: observing, the phenomenon of the observer, consciousness, awareness, and the relationship these have to each other, to learning, and to helping ourselves and others. The bugger is, I will never really know if I'm doing what you are talking about because it is all a matter of perception.

When you teach class, you continually draw our awareness to specific things: our abs, our breath, or our lower back. These parts of our bodies are always operating, especially our breathing, but we aren't consciously aware of them all of the time. Our bodies can't expend energy everywhere all at once. They do what they do and most of the time we just don't pay much attention. In fact, in Pilates class, I'm always surprised that when we are doing "the bridge," I hold my breath until you remind me to breathe. I'm not consciously aware of doing this until you say something; you shift my attention by saying, "Remember to breathe." In a tenth-grade biology class I visited this week they talked

about involuntary muscles like the heart and the lungs. I'm not convinced this is how I would talk about these muscles. We are not consciously aware of these muscles until there is a big problem, what PCT folks call a lot of error. That, in my mind, does not mean they are involuntary.

Awareness is crucial when it comes to taking more effective control of your life. In PCT, we know that as we live our lives, we gain perceptions at the lower levels moving up the levels by building connected networks of perceptions. Some of these are then stored in our memory as reference perceptions. When I think about this, my mind goes back to the first time I looked into a microscope. It was exciting and frustrating all at the same time. It was fun to see a whole new world that I couldn't see with my naked eye, but I had no clue what I was seeing or what to look for. The same is true when learning anything new — like a foreign language, Pilates, or cooking. When we first begin, we are like babies who, for a while, are experiencing sight as different intensities of light. When we are learning, gaining new perceptions, we aren't always aware of what to pay attention to.

The other night I was talking on the phone to a friend who was born in Puerto Rico, and I was trying to repeat something my son was saying in Spanish. My friend chuckled and pointed out that I had said it with no Spanish accent. My untrained ears didn't register that I hadn't spoken with the correct accent. I didn't know what specific perceptions to control for. If I were learning Spanish, over time I would learn to hear the subtle differences that native speakers hear.

There is a great example of this idea of gaining and retaining perceptions in one of my favorite video clips about brain research. It is about a study of babies and the brain. All babies, no matter where they are being raised, can clearly distinguish the tonal difference in two different Chinese phonemes until they are about eighteen months old. After that age, babies cannot tell the phonemes apart unless they are regularly around Chinese speaking individuals. The non-Chinese babies' awareness hasn't been focused on distinguishing the difference in the two phonemes. Without awareness, perceptions appear not to be stored in memory. Researchers talk about the loss of this ability as the pruning of neural networks. The babies who could distinguish the phonemes show how awareness and perception work in concert. In each case, the learner had to first be able to perceive a distinct piece of information by creating a neural signal or connecting a group of neural signals for that information. This creation of a neural signal then had to be partnered with awareness. Then a specific reference perception (the exact state the learner wanted the perception to be) could be remembered and later set. We cannot be consciously aware of something we cannot perceive. Bill Powers says, "I suspect, but I cannot prove, that every distinct object of awareness is one such neural current." I didn't hear what my Spanish-speaking friend heard, my lack of accent, so my awareness was not focused on proper pronunciation. I did not develop a perception or attempt at the time to maintain or match an exact reference perception for the pronunciation. At one time, my friend developed perceptions for the pronunciation of what to him is the correct Spanish accent. Now he has reference perceptions, very specific "just right" sounds he controls for when he hears someone speaking Spanish. When listening to me, his awareness was focused on that particular reference perception. When what I said didn't match his reference perception for the correct accent, BAM!, he experienced error. For me there is no error because I don't hear what I'm mispronouncing. I think that much of learning is about this combination of awareness and perception. In *Behavior: The Control of Perception*, Bill

Powers writes, "The perception is conscious if there is reason to believe that awareness is involved also."

Perception + Awareness = Consciousness

Back to Pilates. Let's look at "zip and hollow." In your class, you want to be able to say one phrase — "zip and hollow" — and have us control our entire abdominal area in very specific ways. Each of us in the class has to be able to perceive the muscle tensions you are asking us to control for. You try to help us by calling on perceptions that we may already have, like stopping our flow of pee, squeezing our butt muscles, or pulling in our ribs. Over time, we can perceive all of the combined muscle tensions you are talking about when you say "zip and hollow." Only then are you able to draw our awareness to a very specific reference perception (which is really a combination of several lower level perceptions) simply by saying "remember zip and hollow." We all find it funny in class when suddenly someone gains a new perception. It is usually followed by an "Ohhh... it never felt like that before." Or someone saying, "You never said that before," even though you have probably said it hundreds of times. Once we perceive something, we can set a reference perception for it. This reference perception is a "just right" condition, a goal, a desired state, or a target. It's a specific remembered perceptual state. Once we perceive all of the muscle tensions required for "zip and hollow," in essence we have gained a new perception. Then the next time you give that direction, we shift our awareness to that reference perception and create the desired muscle tension. Keep in mind that we aren't telling our system what to do, we are experiencing the effects of our actions. We don't tell our neurons to fire, we don't tell a muscle to increase tension by 50 percent, we just feel the aftereffects of our actions as tension in our muscles.

This capability of living systems to shift awareness is a wonderful thing. As you are reading this, I can probably have you shift your awareness by using a key technique based on the principle that *awareness follows error*. Let's give it a try: Are you thirsty? Have you been sitting too long? How do you feel about your mother? What's your favorite song? Tell me one word you would like people to say when they describe you? Are your feet sore? Did your attention shift from the discussion of awareness? Were you shifting the flashlight all over your system? These questions encourage you to scan your system for error, and it is a basic tenet of PCT that awareness follows error. This ability to shift awareness is very important. In a difficult situation, shifting my awareness to the person I want to be can be really helpful.

I did this a lot during my divorce. A counseling friend, Shelley Brierley, asked me once, "What lessons do you want to teach your sons about how women deal with difficult situations?" This question shifted my awareness from the immediate situation to the kind of parent I wanted to be. Once I was controlling for being the kind of parent I wanted to be, a whole lot of other things fell into place. I was better able to model for my sons how to deal with difficult situations. I'm not saying this was easy. To be totally honest, some days it was nearly impossible. However, drawing my awareness to the lessons I was teaching my sons helped. Shifting awareness is one of those ideas that is easy to say and hard to do. The more error we are experiencing, the more difficult shifting our awareness becomes. Kind of like when holding the flashlight on a specific object becomes more difficult as our muscles become fatigued.

Shifting our awareness intentionally and in a specific direction is difficult for several reasons. First, awareness

follows error. Being complex creatures, the chance we are running error somewhere in the system is very likely. Second, there is always a lot of noise in the environment, information we need to filter out, much like static on a radio. We are bombarded with thousands of data each second; it is amazing hat we don't overload our circuits. This might be why the average person has an attention span of 6 to 10 seconds. I find it helpful to think of awareness, as described by some scientists, as a series of "now moments" in which we hold onto an idea or thought and change almost as quickly as we can say the words Now-Now-Now. With our awareness flashlight moving constantly, is it any wonder we have difficulty consciously shifting our awareness? There are a few practices that can help. We both practice some form of meditation to help us have more conscious control over our awareness. Dr. Joe Dispenza in *What the Bleep Do We Know?* puts it this way: "Consciousness is moving through the brain, and using the brain to examine the options and possibilities." Through meditation we begin to use the brain to move consciousness. Right now, try to sit quietly, and see how long you can go before a different thought floats by. As with most things, the more we practice, the easier it becomes.

I recently listened to the audiobook *The Art of Mindful Living* by Thich Nhat Hanh. In the beginning, we are told that as we listen, we will periodically hear a bell. It is the bell of mindfulness and it is rung to "remind participants of their true nature and to return to their breathing." The bell ringing, remembering to zip and hollow, or asking questions are all ways to shift awareness in the system. The narrator asks that when we hear the bell, we focus our attention on our breathing, being aware of the present moment. I have learned a very valuable lesson from better understanding behavior: I can only live from this moment

on. I cannot change the past, and I don't have much control over the future. What I am better at now is living in this moment and being aware of who I want to be in the present, which leads me to be more of who I want to be in the future.

Awareness, observation, and consciousness are all tangled up together, so intertwined that we sometimes can't separate them. It is interesting to me that sometimes what someone else notices about me is something that I am not aware of. When I was teaching eighth grade, I once asked a student to imitate me, and the result was hilarious. I found out a lot about myself, much as I did the first time I watched myself on video giving a presentation. We all do this, notice things about others that they are unaware of. The key here is to intentionally use observation to be helpful, not hurtful. I'm not talking here about "constructive criticism," to me there is no such thing. The word criticism means disapproval. I'm talking about only sharing observations just as if we are the tape recorder or the video camera.

For example, I've noticed that you sometimes twist your hair around your finger (this is an observation). If I say, "Twilight, I believe you twist your hair when you are nervous or in turmoil," then I'm being judgmental (expressing an opinion). Often times people aren't even aware of habits such as fiddling with their hair or biting their nails; these are unconscious actions. If I were trying to help you, I may see your hair twisting as a potential signal that something else is going on inside of you — what I think of as a disruption signaling a thought behind the thought. This idea of observing — watching for such disruptions — is very important for counselors and others in helping professions. The observation in and of itself isn't helpful or hurtful. However, how we express the observation and our intent in expressing it can be helpful or hurtful.

Sometimes our observations can be hurtful even though we might think we are acting in other's best interests. I think this happens most often when these observations are intended to judge people or their actions. William Glasser is often quoted as saying, "Happy people evaluate themselves, unhappy people evaluate others." When I find myself observing others in this way, I try to be reflective and realize that what I'm observing is really probably more about me than them. Remember, it's all about me! When I look at others and their actions, and when I hear that voice in my head being judgmental, I think about what Glasser had to say and ask myself, "What is it I'm seeing in this person that is reflective of who I am?" I've learned to think of these moments as glimpses of my shadow. Just as in a painting, my shadow is there to show depth. When my focus shifts to me and what I can control, I let go of trying to control or judge others.

The idea of recognizing ourselves as we look at others is everywhere these days. Betsy Chasse in *What the Bleep Do We Know?* says it this way: "I've found if I can't put a finger on my emotional state — look around me, it's reflecting right back at me." Kent Nerburn in *Small Graces* talks about it as the gift of the echo:

> Gradually I came to look upon [the] echo as my teacher. To listen to that echo was to hear myself in the way that others heard me — not my thoughts and ideas, but the plainsong of my heart.
>
> A tinge of anger, an air of sadness, a catch in my throat, a tone too shrill — all the truths I tried to hide were present in that echo. It is the mirror of my spirit...
>
> I still listen constantly for the music beneath the words of common speech. But, more than that, I try

always to look upon the world and the people I meet as the echoes of my spirit. I know that if I am speaking with deceit, deceit will be echoed back to me. If I am acting with anger, the echo of that anger will return to me in the words and actions of others.

Likewise, if I find that I am constantly cheerful, full of brightness and hope, or deeply contemplative in the presence of a particular person ... I am echoing the gift that is being given to me. It is as if the lesson of the echo contains the secret to understanding the space between us all.

The more I understand PCT the more I understand that if I focus my awareness on not only what's going on, but what inside of me is shaping my understanding of what's going on, I am able to take more effective control of my life. In that moment when I take a step back and look inside at what's shaping my understanding I bring into play the *phenomenon of the observer*. There appears to be within each of us the ability to observe ourselves as if we are looking from a different point of view, like we are watching a play in which we are one of the actors.

This whole arena of awareness, consciousness, observing and the phenomenon of the observer fascinates me, probably because I love to learn, and these are topics that scientists today are trying to better understand. One of my favorite quotes about awareness and consciousness is from Philip Runkel's *People as Living Things: The Psychology of Perceptual Control.* Writing about awareness, he quotes Bill Powers as saying:

> There is one core that remains the same no matter what the content of consciousness: the silent Observer... The watcher of the screen on which experience

appears... The point of view. There is always a point of view of which you're not aware but from which you are aware... Why are you not aware of the pressure of the seat you're sitting in until I mention it? Because the sensory endings were not responding? Not at all. The signals were there all along. But the overseer was looking elsewhere in the hierarchy."

Powers's idea of "the observer," what I call here "the phenomenon of the observer," helps us understand how to take more effective control of our lives and how to help others. It helps us understand that in the midst of what is going on, we cannot remove ourselves. It reminds me of the movie *The Neverending Story* in 'which the main character in the movie becomes part of the story he is reading. At times, we must pause and try to step out of our own story for a moment. We must observe our own system as if we are watching a movie, as if we were not a part of the movie.

When it comes to being the observer I have to remember that when I observe others, I cannot separate myself from my observations. And when I am trying to observe myself, I am attempting to somehow take a step back and watch as if I am not involved.

When helping others we attempt to be this separate, take-a-step-back observer for them. The helper watches for subtle changes in actions, pace, tone, or topic — for example, if I observe you twisting your hair. These subtle changes can be an indicator of disruptions and an opportunity to ask a question and hopefully shift your awareness somewhere else. As the helper I'm trying to help you *bump it up*. I'm trying to help you go up a level, take a step back and watch, by having you explore your background thoughts. By looking at the problem from a higher level you may be able to resolve what you are working on. I like to think of the hierarchy of

control loops as being much like an old-fashioned telephone switch board. It is as if all of the loops are controlling. One starts flashing, and our system's awareness shifts to that one. One of the problems with this analogy is we are being rewired all the time. What I call "flashing" is awareness moving toward error. Remember, error occurs when there is a mismatch between a reference (something I want) and a perception (what I'm recording). Awareness follows error. It is this ability to shift our awareness that helps us help each other and ourselves. If we can shift our awareness to the "right" flashing light, we can reduce the error and move on. Usually the *flashing light* is error at a higher level.

For example, let's say you are talking about something in your life that isn't the way you want it to be right now. For example when you first started dating your current boyfriend, but were still thinking a lot about your previous boyfriend, your thoughts flowed from one topic to another, and suddenly you said, "I know my mother thinks the right thing to do is to walk away. *I just can't do that!*" At that point, I might ask, "Right then when you said 'I just can't do that?' what were you thinking?" Often these little interruptions are indicators of a background thought, and by asking you a question, I can sometimes help you shift your awareness to the background thought. This is what I mean by bumping it up, shifting awareness to a higher level where the conflict can be resolved.

In the novel *The Valkyries*, author Paulo Coelho talks about the idea that we have foreground and background thoughts going on at the same time. Coelho refers to the background thoughts as our *second mind*. We can help ourselves by taking time to bring this second mind to our conscious awareness. We can figuratively take a step back and become our own observer. When we try to help others we want to help them do this for themselves. We want to

remember to get out of other people's way and not interfere as they help themselves. Too often we get wrapped up in the drama, or the content of what people are telling us, and forget to watch for the flashing light and explore what's behind their thoughts.

Folks who understand PCT assume those they are helping have the answers for themselves. In *Method of Levels*, Tim Carey says, "Our job (as the helper) is to ask about whatever is on their mind, and then ask about background thoughts whenever we pick up on a disruption that has occurred." I think of "helping" someone as helping that person shift awareness. Like the switchboard operator, I watch for the flashing lights and plug the person in, connecting her to another part of herself.

I think it is important to remember that the ideas of awareness, observing, the phenomenon of the observer, and consciousness are ideas being explored by cutting-edge scientists in many fields of study, from art to metaphysics. It is humbling to realize that although mankind has made quantum leaps in understanding the physical sciences, the mind and consciousness are the new frontiers to explore. Knowing that we don't have all the answers and living in the present moment can serve each of us well. As Fred Alan Wolf, a quantum physicist, is fond of saying, "Be in the mystery!"

Keep exploring your second mind.

In a nutshell

- Perception is a prerequisite of consciousness and awareness.

- Perception and awareness are both requirements of consciousness.

- Humans have the ability to shift their awareness.

- Humans have the ability to act as their own observer.

- People have both foreground and background thoughts.

- Helping means getting out of the way of the other person's thought process and not getting caught up in the drama of the story.

- We cannot change the past nor can we control the future; staying focused in the present is where we have the most control.

- Learning to consciously shift our awareness can help us take more effective control of our lives.

- Without awareness, perceptions appear not to be stored in memory.

CHAPTER 9

Dear Linda,

Relationships, conflict, and disturbance

About five years ago, one of the women I go to the gym with on a regular basis asked me if I would be willing to talk with her sister-in-law, Linda, who was dealing with a difficult situation. For weeks I tried getting together with Linda, and it just didn't seem to work. Then one day we were both at the gym and I invited her to go to McDonald's with me for breakfast.

We began to regularly visit McDonalds after the gym, and over the years we have become great friends. Linda and I share a lot in common. During the five years of our friendship we have lived through many changes together, including her divorce and selling her home. My youngest son and her oldest son have become good friends. Her daughter has become the daughter I never had.

Linda is a frequent reminder to me that although we have many experiences in common, we do not see them the same way because of who we are. There are times when I call on her and say, "I need to talk with someone. Can you meet me for breakfast?" And there are times when she calls on me. Both of us have a genuine curiosity about people, how they think, what they believe, and how they act. At one point we spent our mornings reading from a book my son refers to as The McDonald's Book. *(The actually title is* Kokology: The Game of Self-Discovery *by Tadahiko Nagao and Isamu Saito.) It is a book with short question and vignettes to help you explore your inner space, and reading through it together with Linda was a great way to get to know each other.*

Through helping her, I have learned to take the technical aspects of Perceptual Control Theory and put them into common practical language and experience. In this way, she has been my teacher. Many of our breakfast discussions have centered on our difficulties in personal relationships. The greatest bonds of friendship may be formed not by how we are alike, but by how we balance and blend our differences.

Dear Linda,

Spending time with you at McDonalds in the morning is always fun and thought-provoking. I often think about how our common experience of being married to and now divorced from law enforcement officers has brought us together. Whenever people share a similar experience, they can build bridges more quickly. Overlapping topics that seem to keep coming up in our conversations are relationships and conflict, probably because we have a tendency to focus on what's not working. Writing is a way I pull my thoughts together, so I thought it might be helpful if I capture on paper some of what we have talked about in terms of how we can prevent problems from arising between two control systems (two people), and how we might be able to resolve conflicts with others while taking care of ourselves.

Perry Good, a friend who teaches with me, talks about how Perceptual Control Theory is just plain common sense, but the problem is that sometimes plain common sense becomes available to you five minutes after you really need it. What I'm hoping to do is help you access your plain common sense more often, in the moment, when you are in a relationship with someone else. It doesn't matter if the other person is a mother, a daughter, a teacher, a student, a boss, an employee, a friend, a co-worker, or a romantic interest. In all of these cases, we need to remember that we are working with two living control systems with two different "just right" references and two different perceptions. Often these systems are trying to control the same environmental elements at the same time.

So let's take a moment to think a bit differently about "issues" in a relationship. Instead of thinking of these issues as *conflict*, let's try thinking about them as *disturbance*. There are two reasons for thinking in terms of disturbance. First, if we think about the results of another's actions as disturbance, we are less likely to take his action as a personal attack. Second, this thinking usually allows more degrees of freedom, what I think of as more wiggle room, for resolving the issue. When people think of an issue as conflict between individuals, they begin to think of it as an inability for both parties to get what they want. They then try to resolve conflict by having a winner and a loser, or by looking for compromise. In the end, no one really gets what they want. If, however, I understand PCT, and I think about an issue as each person's actions resulting in disturbance to the other, I may figure out a way for both people to get what they want. Remember, disturbance is any force in the environment that I am not controlling that affects what I want. Thinking about conflict as disturbance may give you more options for action and may help you be more effective. Here's a quick example. There have been times when my mother would visit my house and "pick up and clean" my kitchen. Any two people trying to clean the same room can create an interesting situation, an issue. From my perspective, I wanted a clean kitchen, and she was a force in the environment over which I had no control. I could have thought of us as being in conflict. But because I understand PCT, I tried to think of her as disturbance. The question then became, was she a facilitating or a hindering force, and most often, the answer from my perspective was that she was both. If I thought in terms of conflict, I could have spent all of my time thinking, "Mom would you just get out

of here! This is my house and you're not helping." (I win.) Or "Let it go, Shelley. She will be gone in a day or two anyway." (I lose.) or "Okay you go ahead and clean the cupboards, and I'll take care of the fridge." (We both give a little, compromise.) But when I viewed her actions as disturbance, I realized "the issue" was all about me, and not her. It wasn't that we couldn't both get what we wanted. We just needed to approach the situation in a whole different way. In other words, I needed to *bump it up*! If I focused on what type of a daughter I wanted to be, I'd be looking at the situation from a higher level reference. I then might ask my mother, "What can I do to help?" I want to be a daughter that is helpful to her mother, just as I want to model for my sons how to be helpful to their mother (a.k.a. me). Thinking of it as disturbance also helps me focus on what am I controlling for at this moment. What do I really want? This isn't about what my mother is doing, (remember IJI — it's just information); it is about what I'm controlling for and how I'm recording what's happening. Thinking in terms of disturbance reminds me that what she is doing might be seen as helpful, rather than hindering. It may mean I don't have to smell burning crumbs every time I use my toaster. You get the idea. Most importantly, thinking in terms of disturbance reminds me that I have no control over my mother.

As you read through the rest of this letter, let this idea of thinking about issues as disturbance rather than conflict percolate in the back of your mind. There are several ways to both prevent and resolve this perceived inability for individuals or groups to get what they want. And much of it involves plain common sense.

The first step in conflict prevention seems so simple, yet my experience tells me that people find it difficult to do. Take better care of yourself and your own system. We are often so busy taking care of everyone else that we neglect ourselves. I've heard the statistic that one in four Americans suffer from some form of depression. People's brains are inflamed by an influx of stress hormones, and when individuals don't attend to some simple healthy habits we run the risk of disease, either mental or physical. In PCT terms, a system in error is going to produce output intended to decrease error. So when our systems are stressed, we secrete hormones intended to decrease this error. Over time, too much of anything will take a toll on our bodies. Psychiatrist Henry Emmons recommends taking some simple actions to better care for ourselves. He calls these actions the triad of health.

* **Diet:** eat organic, pay attention to the types of fats in foods, and monitor vitamin and mineral intake. A February 2000 study in the *Journal of Alternative and Complementary Medicine* found that in children ages 6 to 12 either a well-balanced diet or low-dose vitamin-mineral supplements improves brain function and subsequently lowers institutional violence and antisocial behavior by almost half. Proper nutrition is essential to taking better care of your own system.

* **Physical activity:** participate in a well-balanced fitness regime.

* **Sleep:** get seven to eight hours of rest a night. Much brain research discusses a body's natural biorhythm. The peak of the cycle is mid-way between sunrise and sunset. When we do not get enough rest, our bodies begin to release more stress hormones.

Think about what you can do in your life to take better care of yourself. A simple technique for reducing stress that I find helpful is to take a couple of hours during a hectic

week to go to the movies. It seems that the sillier and more predictable the movie is, the better it works to help me let go of stress and re-energize. You've heard people say that the most important person to have a good relationship with is yourself because you'll always be there. Well that's the idea here; be a friend to yourself first. The trick is to do enough self-friending without becoming self-absorbed.

Have you ever noticed that on days when you truly feel at peace, the outside world doesn't seem to have much of an effect on you? For example, on days when I'm aware of myself and taking care of myself, my boys can get into a fuss at the dinner table, and I don't much notice and don't much care. But on days when I have been rushing from one thing to another and still want to accomplish three more things before going to bed, they can say very little and I'm really bothered. In PCT terms, I'm running a whole lot of error. When I was a classroom teacher, on days like the latter, the students would often say, "Today isn't a day to mess with Ms. Roy." People who know us well can sense when we are already running error. Some will take advantage of that for their own gain, and others will not attempt to hinder the system more.

Common sense tells us that before we even start to get involved with another person, we need to make sure we are taking care of ourselves. Unfortunately, I see a lot of people around me trying to take care of themselves by getting more involved in "stuff": relationships, activities, work. They seem to think that someone or something outside of them is going to fill them up inside. Filling our lives with things outside of us often increases error rather than decreases it. It's a practice that gives us more issues to cope with rather than fewer, and more stress rather than less. We often do the opposite of what would help the most. As my mother was fond of saying, "An ounce of prevention is worth a pound of cure." To reduce or prevent hindering disturbance in a relationship, make sure you are doing what it takes to keep your own system as error-free as possible.

In addition, it's important to remember that in general the external world is not the cause of what happens inside of us. What's "out there" is, in most cases, neutral. When we are in a relationship, we often think that it is what the other person says or does that creates issues, and that if they would just stop doing or saying "the wrong thing," life would be wonderful. When I work to resolve conflict between two parties, much of my time is spent getting both parties to realize that it isn't about the other person. Linda, I know I sometimes fall into this trap myself. "If Wesley really cared about me, he would pick up after himself." What I need to realize is that "picking up" is *my* way of showing I care, not Wesley's. For him, the two may have nothing to do with each other. If I understand PCT and operate in congruence with what it teaches, I realize that looking outside of myself probably isn't very helpful in reducing stress and internal error. As Fred Allen Wolf puts it, "There is no 'out there' out there, independent of what's going on 'in here.'" It really is all about my own system.

An important way to take care of yourself is to figure out how to reduce as much error as possible in your own system, and how to reduce it as quickly as possible. Effectively resolving conflict doesn't create more error somewhere else. In other words, we want to reduce error, get ourselves under control, without creating more error somewhere else in our own system. This course of action isn't always easy, and it takes a great deal of self-discipline. When we are personally under stress, running a high degree of error ourselves, being aware of and reducing error becomes more difficult. You have heard people suggest count to ten, take three deep breaths, walk away and come back "in control," ask yourself

whether it really matters, and so on. In PCT terms, many of these ideas are intended to reduce error in your own system before trying to interact with someone else.

I find that using PCT language and thinking that both parties are acting as disturbance to each other helps me reduce error and be more aware of my own system. I say to myself, "This is about me, not her." And "What is it that I really want on a higher level right now?" In the moment, just being aware of my own system and taking more effective control helps me deal with situations in which both of us are disturbing each other. If you change your basic understanding at a high level, then much of what I'm saying here will make more sense and be easier to access under stress.

A friend of mine is fond of quoting an old African Proverb; "If there is no enemy within, the enemy outside can do us no harm." This is a good reminder to take care of yourself. Remember that everything outside of yourself is just information (a bunch of noise). You can only control yourself, so reducing your own error is one of the most effective things you can do. My son Duncan puts it this way in talking to his brother, "Wesley, today I'm not going to let you push my buttons, no matter how hard you try."

Another bit of plain common sense when it comes to relationships is to be very clear on what we really want in a given situation. Sometimes being clear on what we want at a higher level of perception can simply dissolve a perceived conflict. There is an old story often told in conflict resolution courses about two people who appear to be in conflict, both wanting the same thing, a shipment of oranges. The argument over who is going to get the shipment is long and involved because both parties feel they have very legitimate reasons for wanting the oranges. In one version, one individual is trying to cure a deadly disease and the other is trying to feed the poor. At the end of the story, we discover that they could both get what they want. The doctor looking for the cure wanted the skin of the oranges, and the social worker wanted the meat of the oranges. Too often in relationships, we do not explore what the other person wants. We think we know each other so well that we don't need to ask, "What is it you want?" We assume we know.

As a single mother, I would sometimes worry about not preparing and eating a home-cooked meal with my sons at the end of every day. One day I asked my sons what they wanted to do about dinner, and they suggested an idea that I never would have suspected. They suggested and from then on we instituted "Fend For Yourself," a night when we each take care of preparing our own food. There's only one rule: Clean up your own mess. I'd been thinking that my boys really wanted me to cook every night, and I found out that they liked the freedom that came from everybody eating what they wanted, at least once in a while. As an added bonus, both of them have learned to cook a few different things. We still do eat as a family several nights a week. It's good for building relationships.

If you think about both the story of the oranges and the one about me and my sons, they demonstrate a lack of effective communication rather than conflict. A colleague once taught me that most conflict between people really means someone doesn't have enough information. Think about that statement for a minute. I find myself in that kind of situation fairly often. For example, a couple of weeks ago, I was upset that a friend of mine hadn't called. I thought we had an agreement that he would call on a certain day, and then he didn't. I didn't hear from him for two or three days. I was angry and upset, and I felt very justified in feeling that way. Some people would say we were in conflict. Then I found out his mother's companion of ten years had passed away, and he had been off helping her. Boy, did I feel like a heel, because in the end I realized I became angry before I had all the important information. So when you think you are "in conflict," it is really important to make sure that you know exactly what both people want and that everyone involved has all of the information. This is just plain common sense, right? And it is another great reason to *ask, don't tell.* I find that if we keep asking until we are both really clear on what we each want, the conflict often disappears.

It's just plain common sense that practicing effective communication skills is essential to good relationships. These skills are the key to building connections, especially in times of perceived conflict. If there is a possibility that what I am about to say or do may disconnect me from someone I want to be connected to in my life, I know I need to employ every effective communication tool in my repertoire, and I need to end the talk with some form of reconnecting. Here's a quick example. If I am going to talk with my son Duncan about changing plans at the last minute, which I know he has a difficult time dealing with, I employ every communication skill I have, and I make sure that at the end of the conversation we talk about something that is important to him or that we do something to strengthen our relationship.

Probably the most commonly known research on communication is that over 55 percent of the message comes from non-verbal information, whereas words only make up about 7 percent of the message and the rest is based on tone and pacing. You have probably already heard the recommendation to use "I" statements rather than "you" and "they" when communicating with someone you are in conflict with. This makes sense when you remember that we can only control ourselves. When I start by saying "You should..." or "When you did ..." I'm not operating based on my understanding of PCT.

A communication key you may not be as familiar with is the idea that there are five components essential for two individuals to walk away from a contentious conversation both feeling they have connected and been understood: sense data, thoughts, feelings, wants, and actions.* You can think of *sense data* as "just the facts." *Thoughts* are the assumption we make based on the facts in front of us. *Feelings* are our emotions, often contradictory, for example during major events in life we often are excited and frightened at the same time. *Wants* for myself, others, and the two of us together keep these unconditional. The last component is actions — past, present, and future. The PCT *action* focus would be on what in the future I will be controlling for. When the present and the past are referenced, they serve as experiences of what hasn't been working.

Key question I can ask myself when trying to communicate effectively with others are: "What am I controlling for here?" and keep trying to bump it up by going for the thought behind the thought. I will sometimes ask myself questions like: What am I trying to protect? What do I want? If I had that, what would be better? If I had that, what would that say about me? What do I want for this person? What do I want for us together?

My last communication recommendation completes the circle. Try to give up the idea that one person is right and the other person is wrong. When you do find yourself thinking this way, ask yourself: Who holds the bag of truth? If you really understand PCT, you know that everyone has his or her own "truth." We all want different things, and we all see

---

* For a lot more information on this, see *Connecting with Self and Others* by Sherod Miller, Daniel Wackman, Elam Nunnally, and Phyllis Miller.

the world through different lenses. Sometimes we both want to control the same thing, and we can't. That's more common sense! It is really hard for parents to remember that our children live in their own worlds, not ours, so we don't know their truth. My Dad worked in the computer industry when it began. I can't tell you how many times he said to me, "I'll never understand why someone would want one of those things [computers] in their house." That was his truth. Well, the truth for me today is that not only do I want a computer in my house, I have four in my house, and I just bought a new one in the middle of writing this book. Powers often points out that what most people view as conflict arises from one person trying to control another. He describes it further by saying conflict between people occurs when the action I take to get what I want prevents you from getting what you want. Here's an example: sometimes I try to "make" my sons clean up the kitchen when they want to finish their video game. For them, cleaning up now is preventing them from finishing their game. Until they decide they want to clean up, it isn't going to happen, and the more I try to "make" them, the greater the error in my system and the more disturbance we become to each other (and I don't mean the facilitating kind). So let me recap. Here are some common sense things you might think about when the world is serving disturbance as its main course.

* Take care of yourself; remember the triad of health.

* Be aware of your own system first, and reduce your own error as quickly as possible.

* Be clear on what you want, and find out what the other person wants at the highest level possible.

✳ Make sure everyone has the whole story. Remember, most perceived conflict comes from someone not having enough information.

✳ Practice effective communication skills:
  ✳ Think in terms of connecting.
  ✳ Use "I" and avoid "they" and "you."
  ✳ Give sensory data, thoughts, feeling, wants, and actions (past, present, and future).
  ✳ Pay attention to non-verbal communication.

✳ Let go of the idea that someone holds "the truth" — each person has her own truth. Thinking of issues as *disturbance* rather than *conflict* may help.

The ideas I've already discussed here concerning one-on-one communication are also essential when working in a larger group. In order for a group to work collaboratively, they must share connected references. Individuals need to be clear on what they want, and they need to reach the best agreement possible on a few key references before they run into problems. This is big picture disturbance prevention involving not just you, but everyone involved in the relationship. In workshops, I often take a large piece of chart paper and put it on the floor. Then I grab a bunch of objects — coins, Popsicle sticks, paper clips, whatever I have handy — and toss these toward the piece of paper. Some land on the paper. Some are close to each other. Some are scattered close to the edge of the paper, and some aren't anywhere near the paper. I then go on to identify this display as symbolizing people in a classroom, a business, an organization, or a society. The piece of paper represents the idea of "being on the same page." The objects represent individuals in a group. It doesn't take people long to realize that if more of

us are on the same page, or if you and I have more references that are similar, the less disturbance, error, and conflict we are going to experience.

This is what I mean by connecting references. You and I can't share a perception or a reference. I can't see for you, I can't hear for you, I can't record your neural signals, I can't set your "just right." But through dialog, we can often come close to connecting or agreeing on wants and desires. This connection appears to be more easily accomplished the higher we go up the levels, maybe because there are fewer perceptions at the higher levels or maybe because they are more universal in nature. This idea of connecting references at a higher level goes back to the time of the ancient Greeks who sought to discover universal principles of ethical behavior. Sometimes, when two people share similar experiences, they naturally connect references. This is why friends and I who grew up in the same neighborhood and during the same time period control for a lot of the same things. It's why you and I have some similar reference perceptions — we've both been married to and divorced from law enforcement officers, both of us are mothers with two children, and we were both born and raised in Minnesota at about the same time.

Scientific literature sometimes refers to connecting references as *collective thought* or *group think*. Dean Radin in *Entangled Minds: Extrasensory Experiences in a Quantum Reality* has experimented with the idea that in some ways when we focus our thoughts are all connected. Jeffrey Satinover in *The Quantum Brain: The Search for Freedom and the Next Generation of Man* talks about a nested hierarchy in which the smallest unit is protein, the second smallest is the brain region, next comes the individual brain, followed by society, and, finally, human kind. At the core of both of these books on complex systems theory is the suggestion that when we get many people in a group to think along the same lines, it becomes synergistic, producing something greater than the sum of its parts. There appear to be collective *fields of thought* created.

You might be asking "Do we need to agree on everything ahead of time? How would that be possible?" The answers are *no* and *it isn't possible*. We want to start connecting at the higher levels, like the principles level, because the higher levels set the reference signals for the lower levels. When we are working with others, we want to have our discussions at as high a level as possible. It is much easier to agree that we both want to be respectful (a higher level reference), than to agree on the right way to fold a towel (a lower level reference). Once we bump it up and have some higher level agreements, we can then begin to define these agreements in more detail. But when we start by discussing the details at the lower level, we usually experience so much error that we don't move on.

When I was a child, my mother and I used to get into arguments all the time. We didn't argue about higher level issues like honesty, but about all kinds of lower level stuff, like the order in which to wash dishes, how to fold clothes, and the necessity of making my bed. I wish I knew then what I know now. If we had spent more time connecting references at the higher levels, there would have been a lot less conflict. Just the other day, you and I talked about this idea when you were having difficulty with your daughter Megan. As we talked, I kept asking you, "What are the three most important things that you want for Megan during her teenage years?" We also talked about you asking her what her most important wants are. For example, you might say, "You know, Megan, you keep telling me you're a teenager now, and you're right, you are. These next five years can be exciting or a constant battle between us or

anything in between. What do you want?" Most kids do not want a constant battle. They want the teenage years to be filled with exciting times. If that's Megan's answer, you could say: "That's what I want too. Now let's figure out what we want to focus on to get this to happen." When my oldest son and I had this conversation, we decided that the three most important things were: 1) school comes first 2) being part of the family 3) our relationship. This played out in many ways but it got us out of fussing at each other about a lot of little things.

I hope this letter has helped you be more aware of your common sense as much as it has helped me remember to use mine. Now I better understand how important it is for me to stop focusing on everyone else and to start taking better care of myself. Then, when my children really need me, I'll be in a better position to help them.

Take care of yourself. It's one of the best ways to build better relationships!

In a nutshell

- Conflict between people and groups usually grows out of a lack of information or an inability to communicate effectively.

- Interpersonal conflicts between individuals or groups might be better managed if we think about them in terms of being disturbance. In many cases these are hindering forces and usually the result of one person trying to control another.

- Be clear on what you want and your thinking behind it.

- As Stephen Covey says, "Seek first to understand." Know what the other person wants.

- Reducing and preventing error in our own system first can help us be more effective.

- Effective communication skills are critical in personal relationships.

- Connecting references at higher levels reduces the risk of error and conflict.

CHAPTER 10

Dear D.J.,

The secrets of internal conflict

*D*o you have some friends who you can't imagine your life without? Well D.J. is that type of friend to me. We grew up together in the same close-knit neighborhood, went to the same elementary school, and graduated in the same class. We swam together, skated together, trick-or-treated together, played night games together, and did a million other things together. We have known each other's brothers, sisters, parents, and many of each other's extended family members. I can't begin to tell you how many hours, memories, and adventures we have shared over the years. Some of these, I wouldn't want to describe in print, and others always bring a smile to my face and give me a good feeling, like the mannequin we had that we dressed up and took to every event during high school and my first years of college.

After high school, D.J. waited a year and went into the Navy to become a nuclear engineer. During his basic training, I wrote to him every day. In fact I should probably credit him for my love of letter writing. We have stayed in touch through his years in the Navy, through my years at the university, through his first years in a nuclear plant, through my first year as a teacher, through weddings, the birth of his sons and mine, the deaths of his mother and my father, and my divorce, and we continue to stay in touch today. We have shared all the big events in our lives and many of the small ones.

During the summer of 2005, several old friends of mine, including D.J., got together for a reunion at my cabin where we had celebrated our high school graduation many years before. It was as if time had stood still, that is until we decided to go water skiing. Old bodies don't move in the same ways that young bodies do.

It was during our summer reunion at the cabin that I started talking in detail about what I was working on, the type

of training I had been doing, and some of the ideas for this book. D.J. was very interested in taking the knowledge he has about engineering concepts — control, negative feedback loops, and nested hierarchies — and applying these ideas to self-evaluating and supervising the engineers with whom he works. Over the next couple of months, we corresponded and talked about a couple of the ideas I have shared in the book. D.J. loves the language of Perceptual Control Theory: it fits well into his frame of reference. When I started to write this chapter on "internal conflict," I knew that D.J.'s struggle over the years to better inform the public about nuclear power would be fertile ground for this part of the book.

In fact, when I sent the first draft of this chapter to D.J., I received emails back with specific examples from the plant where he now works. I have included these in this letter about internal conflict.

This is probably the topic that is most important in taking more effective control of your life. We can be our own greatest champion or our own greatest enemy. It's up to each of us to resolve our own internal conflicts.

Dear D.J.,

It is amazing that when we get together after a long time, it feels as if we just saw each other yesterday. For me, part of the comfort of our friendship is that we experienced a lot of growth together. When I look back, I don't know if I would have ever thought that some day you would be a manager at a nuclear plant and I would be an international consultant and author. We have faced many challenges over the years. In a way, that's what I want to talk with you about: the times of growth when we each faced our own internal struggles, the times when we learned the greatest and sometimes most difficult lessons.

In high school, we were each trying to decide, "Who do I want to be when I grow up?" At the same time, we felt grown up and ready to face the challenges of being adults. Now, we are both facing that same period with our sons. This is a time when they are looking to the future, letting go of child-hood, and learning to be responsible adults. At least that's what we hope they're learning. You and I, like our children, are at a turning point. For us, it is the time when our chil-dren are no longer our major focus and our aging parents are depending more and more on us, a time professionally when we are looking back on experiences and forward to the rest of our careers. Throughout this, and to varying de-grees, we have experienced internal conflict — times when we want two things that cannot occur simultaneously. For example, I want my sons to be independent and I want my sons to still depend on me. And in some ways, my sons

want to be independent, and in other ways, they still want to depend on me. I want to feel sated by what I have accomplished in my career, and I want to challenge myself to move in new directions.

Many people think of conflict as what happens *between* folks. I view that as *disturbance* rather than *conflict.* When there is conflict it appears that the other person is keeping them from getting what they want. As I've explained, when we think of conflict between two individuals or groups as disturbance, we can handle it in more effective ways. Internal conflict is much more difficult to handle. In its most difficult forms, it requires the help of someone else.

Let's start with a more technical discussion of internal conflict. In *Behavior: The Control of Perception,* Bill Powers writes, "A person is said to be 'in conflict' when he wants two incompatible goals to be realized at once." I think of this as wanting to go right and left at the same time. Powers goes on to say that "unresolved conflict leads to anxiety, depression, hostility, unrealistic fantasies, and even delusions and hallucinations... In fact as I have come to realize what inner conflict means in terms of this feedback model, I have become more and more convinced that conflict itself, not any particular kind of conflict, represents the most serious kind of malfunction of the brain, short of physical damage, and the most common even among 'normal' people." Thinking about conflict in this way is very different, because it doesn't involve blaming someone else. In fact, it doesn't involve anyone but yourself. Learning to recognize and resolve internal conflict is of great value in taking more effective control of your life. It can help you be a better manager, a better parent, a better partner, and a happier person.

How do we recognize when we are experiencing internal conflict? It is usually accompanied by or expressed as a sense of loss of control. I might say, "I wish I weren't feeling so sad," as if I have no control over my own emotions. Or "My life is such a mess; I just can't seem to get a handle on it." Or I might say, "I really want to go, but I just can't." These are representative of higher level conflicts, which are more difficult and may take longer to resolve. In each case I am expressing two different wants; two simultaneous goals that conflict with each other. Let's take an example and examine it more closely: "I really want to go, but I just can't go." In this case, I want to go somewhere, and I don't want to go. I can't possibly control for both and not run error. When I write it here, it seems a bit crazy to me. But when I'm experiencing it, it seems perfectly rational.

Just this morning, I wanted to invite a good friend to breakfast, and at the same time, I wanted to go to breakfast alone so I could do some reading. For a moment or two I paused and did nothing. This pause can be an indicator that I may be in conflict. I'll bet you've had the same kind of experience. Take a minute and think about it. When are some times in your life when you have wanted two incompatible things at the same time?

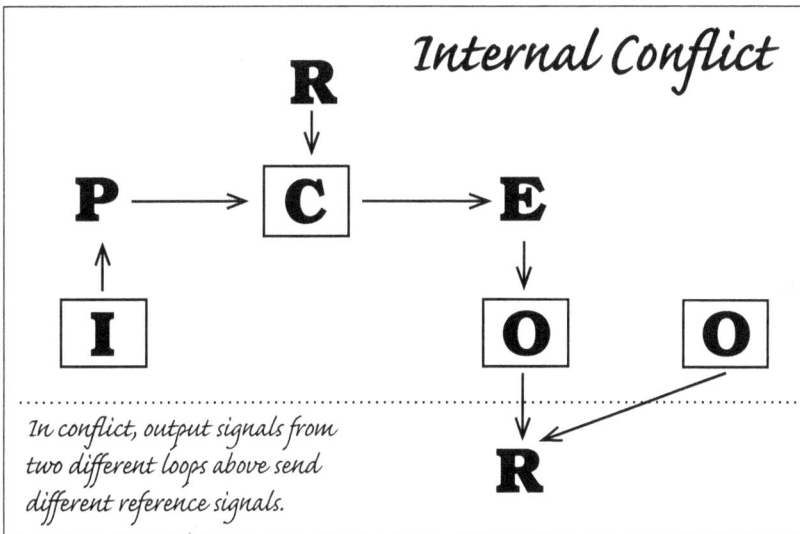

Internal Conflict

In conflict, output signals from two different loops above send different reference signals.

If we took some time to explore each of these examples we would realize that, at the heart of each, the problem is really about wanting two things at the same time, on the same level of perception. To identify the problem, we need to go beyond what we see, think, or hear at the surface level. Scientifically, I mean we need to look higher up the perceptual hierarchy. Take the breakfast example. The conflict was really between being the kind of friend I want to be and being a knowledgeable presenter by finishing the book I've been reading to prepare for a training session. For a moment, I couldn't figure out how to do both. If I can figure out how to do both, then I'm not in conflict. If I decide that one is more important than the other, then I am not in conflict. What sometimes compounds the conflict is that we often try to resolve it by thinking in terms of either/or; either I call my friend or I eat alone and read. This kind of thinking doesn't resolve the conflict; it shifts our awareness to one reference or the other.

Some people would call this awareness shifting "choice," but I struggle with that word. Choice is often thought of as it applies to action. I choose to yell or I choose to walk away. This might be picky thinking on my part, but, as I understand PCT, I do not choose my actions, I choose what I am going to control *for*. My actions are simply a result of my output signals setting references for lower levels all the way down the hierarchy where they activate muscles and glands. I think a better way to express what's happening is to say *my awareness shifts*. I control for something different. If I'm not in agreement with a co-worker, I don't technically choose to yell or to walk away; I control for something such as maintaining a good business relationship with this person. That's the idea behind bumping it up. I shift my awareness to a higher level in the hierarchy, such as the principles level, or I project my possibilities forward in time.

The idea of taking the possibilities forward in time is what I think of as using the imaginary track (in the loop). Using the *imaginary track* around the loop is different from the loop actually operating. Instead of my output going into the environment it stays internal. It is a mental rehearsal, so to speak. In this case, to bump it up, I might try asking, "As a supervisor what do I want to model for this employee?" Or I might project out in time by asking: "What type of a long-term relationship do I want to have with this person?"

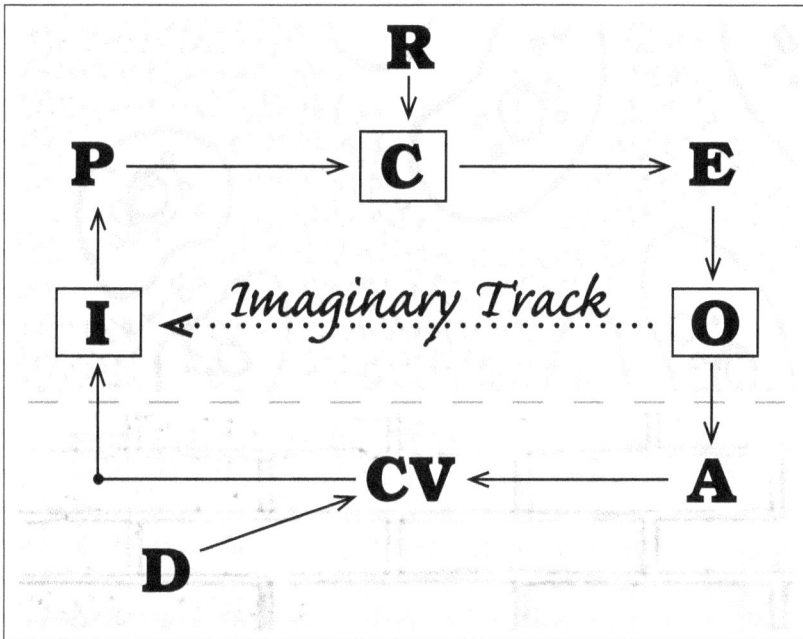

When someone feels out of control, it is often because they are in conflict internally. Others often think that they know what the conflicted person should do, that they know how to "fix it." Remember the last time you said to a friend that you just don't know what to do? My guess is that the friend's reply was a list of actions that she was sure would

work for you. Think of a time when an employee came to you with a problem. How did you try to help? Did you use your wealth of experience and superior knowledge to try to resolve the problem for her?

Do you remember when we were in high school, and our parents and teachers tried to tell us what was in our best interest? When I hear myself talking like that to my sons, I try to remember what that was like when I heard it from my elders. I've decided to give up the "best interest" speeches and, in some ways, that decision is a genuine relief. I don't know how to solve other people's internal conflicts! I am not them, and a solution that would work for me probably won't work for them. This course of action is easy to say but can be hard to do. Fortunately, with practice I'm getting better at it. The answers are within the other person; you can help pull them out, but stop trying to shove your answers into someone else.

I think of these examples as higher level because they are about the system trying to control for references above the program level. I find that with adults these are easier conflicts to spot. Most of us have already learned how to resolve many of our lower level conflicts. If you're wondering if, as we age, we still experience lower level conflicts, the answer is yes. It isn't that lower level conflicts don't occur; they just take less energy and are usually resolved more quickly. That is probably why we don't recognize them as conflicts. For example, let's say I'm picking up all the stuff in my family room that I want to take upstairs (basically operating at the sequence level), and my hands are full. Then I spy one more book that I keep upstairs. Lower level conflict occurs because I can't complete the sequence I was running. I recognize it because there's a slight pause in my actions. I think of this as being like the pause feature on a DVD player. For just a moment I do nothing, until my awareness

shifts to a higher level (the program level), which sets a different reference for the lower levels, and I move into action, no longer executing an ordered sequence of steps. This type of conflict usually comes and goes so quickly that we often don't even recognize it as conflict.

I think this ability to quickly resolve lower level conflict is part of maturation. Sometimes, when you watch young children, you can imagine the wheels turning in their heads when they are faced with internal conflicts. Around age five, many children stop whatever they are doing when they are injured, and you can almost see them thinking, "I want to cry, but I don't want to cry." They will often look to see who is around and then begin to cry or almost magically ignore the injury and move on. If I were to venture a guess about their thinking, I might say that sometime around age five, we gain a higher-level perception about being a big kid, and that perception is linked to crying. As we resolve these lower level conflicts, we gain higher level perceptions and begin to take more effective control of our lives. The more conflict-resolving we do, the better we do it. That's a great reason to let children figure out how to fix it themselves.

In their work on child development, *The Wonder Weeks: How to Turn Your Baby's 8 Great Fussy Phases into Magical Leaps Forward*, Frans Plooij and Hetty Vanderijt outline eight developmental leaps that all babies experience in the first sixty weeks of life. These leaps allow the baby to assimilate information in a new way, to gain new skills, and to grow. They talk about "signs of a leap," which I think of as signs of internal conflict.

"Shortly before each leap, a sudden and extremely rapid change occurs within the baby. It's a change in the nervous system, chiefly the brain, and it may be accompanied by some physical changes as well.

... we call this a 'big change.' Each big change brings the baby a new kind of perception and alters the way that she perceives the world. And each time a new kind of perception swamps your baby, it also brings the means of learning a new set of skills appropriate for that world."

Plooij and Vanderijt refer to these signs as the 3 C's: crying, crankiness, and clinginess. Although the authors are describing children, I think their descriptors fit most adults as well when they are trying to resolve internal conflicts. If you find yourself hanging on to something, not wanting to let go of an idea or an object or a relationship (clinging), or if you are crying a lot or really cranky or moody, it might help to realize that you may be in conflict. Like a baby, you may be ready to gain a new perception and learn a whole new way to operate in the world. Sometimes just recognizing this and seeing your present state in this way helps you experience less stress or pain. Here's a way to help you remember this concept:

Clinging + Crankiness + Crying = Conflict

Conflict Resolution = Growth

Tim Carey in *Method of Levels* says, "A person's behaviors, thoughts, or feelings are never the problem. The only psychological problem is the degree to which a person experiences distress about particular behaviors, thoughts, or feelings." Not making the bed in the morning is only a problem if you find yourself not making the bed and wanting the bed made. We may be more aware of higher-level conflicts because of the amount of distress we experience and the

length of time it takes to resolve them. Philip Runkel sums it up nicely in *People as Living Things*. He talks about these parameters of internal conflict:

* Lower level controls are called upon to control for two different references.

* The person in internal conflict experiences emotional turmoil.

* A higher level reference is required to resolve the conflict.

In popular movies today, there are many examples of people dealing with and trying to resolve internal conflict. In the movie *Save the Last Dance*, Derek (Sean Patrick Thomas), who has talent and street smarts, has to deal with his friend Malakai (Fredro Starr), who is still deep in the thug life Derek is trying to avoid. At one point Derek is faced with "owing his friend" who went to jail for him or doing what he believes will help him realize his dream of becoming a doctor. The question, "How can one be true to himself and true to his friends at the same time?" is a great illustration of a high level internal conflict. Another movie that is full of internal conflict is *Erin Brockovich*. Erin (Julia Roberts) discovers a systematic cover-up of the industrial poisoning of a city's water supply, which threatens the health of the entire community. While conducting her investigation, she finds herself leaving her own children to be taken care of by a friend. She struggles with this issue through much of the movie, until she realizes that she is trying to help many other people's children and by doing so will also help her own. Several other characters in the film face internal conflicts when asked to bring evidence

against a company for which they work and toward which they feel loyalty.

Such moral dilemmas are all examples of internal conflicts at the principles or systems level. Take a minute and see if you can think of a few others. Remember that internal conflict is not about right versus wrong. It is not a matter of being morally correct, obeying the law, or judging someone else's ethics. Internal conflict is always about higher level systems wanting a system one lower level to control for two different things at the same time.

There are always three levels of control operating during internal conflict. In the movie *Erin Brockovich,* an employee of Pacific Gas and Electric has a memo that can be used as evidence against the company. Let's start at the lower level, the level at which the conflict is expressed. In this case, he keeps the memo and warns his family and friends. The next higher level is that at which the conflict is created. We might think of this as the level for setting two references, one for talking and one for not talking. And the highest level is that at which the conflict has the possibility of being resolved. Remember, recognizing internal conflict isn't always easy.

You might be asking yourself, "How does this help me the next time I'm dealing with a troubling issue?" First, realize the conflict is about you and no one else. Second, test yourself to see if the problem is an internal conflict as I've described it above. I usually do this by shoving my thinking to one side and then the other and seeing what feels right. If one side feels more right than the other, I'm probably not in conflict. Some folks make a list of positives and negatives and weigh them against each other. This sounds like an easy process, but when you are faced with a major issue, a true internal conflict, it won't be easy. Another way of testing for internal conflict is to think of the situation in terms of "or." "Or" thinking is something we get trapped into all the

time; either I like you *or* I don't, either I'm good *or* I'm bad. Either it is yes *or* it is no. If one of these works, and *feels just right* then it probably isn't a case of internal conflict. It was just a case of you taking time at one level to set a reference for lower levels. One problem I personally still struggle with is being generous *and* setting boundaries. The solution isn't in being generous *or* setting boundaries. It is in doing both, setting boundaries *and* being generous.

If an issue you are dealing with feels like an internal conflict, I have two suggestions. First, see if you can find an "and" solution. There have been times when I felt I have been both generous *and* set boundaries. Second, get help! I mean this. Many high level internal conflicts require the help of a trained professional. If you find that you are depressed, have long-term anxiety, or have a feeling of being "out of control" for a long period of time, these are all indicators that you may need outside help.

Internal Conflict

* Realize it's about you and no one else.

* Test to see if it truly is internal conflict.

* Look for an "and" solution.

* Get outside help, professional help if necessary.

My bias would be to get help from someone who under-stands PCT and uses something called the Method of Levels, which is based on the idea of exploring the thought behind your thinking. Tim Carey has written a book on using this approach titled *Method of Levels: How to Do Psychotherapy Without Getting in the Way.*

The premise here is that at any given moment you have a foreground thought and a background thought. Someone experienced in PCT will watch for disruptions as you talk and help you explore the thought behind what you are say-ing. When PCT practitioners notice disruptions — such as a sudden outburst or a nervous tick, they might ask, "What's that about?" For example, when I hear myself say, "I'll have to come back and write this part later," I'll ask what that is all about. Well, I want to write something that will make sense. So what's that all about? It's about me creating something that helps people better understand PCT. So what's that all about? That's about me wanting to help others. I could keep going, but you get the idea. This self-questioning may be helpful, but it sometimes takes another individual to ob-serve you as you are talking. There seems to be something about having to verbalize your thinking out loud that helps clarify your thinking. The person watching then looks for disruptions often missed by the individual talking. When we are in conflict, we are usually very focused on the content of the issue, and someone employing the Method of Levels will be an active echo, watching for personal signals and not wrapped up in the content of what we are talking about.

When you are supervising others, you can employ some of the same principles. This process of exploring the thought behind the thought may remind you of another process: the Five Why's recommended in *The Fifth Discipline Fieldbook* by Peter Senge, Richard Ross, Bryan Smith, Charlotte Rob-erts, and Art Kleiner. The Five Why's basically reminds us

to keep asking why until we get to a root cause.

"I see your late to work... why?"

"Because my alarm clock didn't go off."

"Why didn't your alarm clock go off?"

"Because I forgot to turn it on."

"Why didn't you turn it on?" and so on.

The difference here is that in PCT we aren't looking for a root cause, instead we are trying to help the individual find the source of the conflict. So here are my recommendations, when you are trying to help someone else in conflict.

Ways to help others in conflict

1   Recognize it's about them, not you.

2   Listen without getting involved or mired in the story or the content of the issue. This is really tough, especially when what they are saying is something you have experienced yourself or is something you are paid to be in control of.

3   Listen for an idea, belief, or principle behind what they are saying.

4   Explore what's behind what they are saying. The solution is never the first thing that pops up. Often the solution won't occur to them for days, but they will usually express the idea that things are much clearer now.

5   Ask the person to try to step outside of himself for a minute, and then see if he can get any closer to resolving the issue. Ask him to talk about himself in the third person if it helps.

6 Ask the stupid questions. What may appear to be obvious usually isn't during conflict.

You recently shared a work story with me that fits in with this idea of asking the "stupid" question to help someone self-evaluate. You wrote to me that a technician was in internal conflict because he had been involved in a test that could trip a reactor if done incorrectly, and the reactor tripped at exactly the same time he was performing the test. This individual happens to be a high performer and has not made any significant mistakes in his twenty years at work. He also wants to be accountable for his actions. He was searching for possibilities for why the plant response occurred, and he hoped to find a reason other than the test he was conducting. He wanted the problem to not be his fault. You might ask him, "How do you think your actions affected the reactor?" What is most important in this example is your intent in asking the stupid question. If your intent had been to be judgmental or critical of someone else, the employee wouldn't be encouraged to self-evaluate. The tone of voice and body language we use in these situations are critical to staying aligned to PCT.

Everything I'm talking about here has its roots in systems thinking and the application of systems thinking to working with individuals. Engineers are often well versed in systems thinking and the tools associated with it through their scientific training. Your understanding of how mechanical control systems work can help you better understand how people work in the PCT model. In *The Fifth Discipline Fieldbook*, the authors refer to the discipline of working with *mental models* of individuals and the *ladder of inference* as offering the highest leverage for change. In PCT terms, this involves "bumping it up," exploring the thought behind the

thought, and employing the Method of Levels. Acquiring this skill requires patience and perseverance.

After I wrote to you about of internal conflict and how difficult it can be to resolve, you wrote to me about a personal internal conflict you experienced in your role as supervisor and member of a management team in a nuclear plant. Here are some of the details you provided:

The Context: *Two technicians who worked for me were involved in a periodic test in which they encountered a problem with the test meter they were using. They quickly diagnosed the problem, but in their haste to continue the test, they skipped some of the error minimization steps that we had trained them to use, and they reinserted the meter on the wrong scale (using ohms instead of volts). This created a circuit that tripped the plant, costing the company about $800,000 in recovery costs.*

The Conflict: *I had the responsibility of evaluating the technicians' performance to determine their culpability for purposes of assigning discipline. I gave this much thought and based on much data, I determined that a three-day suspension and some refresher training was appropriate discipline. My senior management team decided, with very little thought and consideration, that a much stiffer penalty was warranted and that these employees might be terminated. As the responsible manager, I ended up signing a letter giving them a ten-day suspension. I have now had to defend my decision through the company's grievance process.*

I needed to, as you say, "bump it up" to resolve within myself the internal conflict between being the

team player I wanted to be (which meant doing what my senior management team thought was right) and the fair manager I wanted to be (which meant doing what I originally thought was right).

Side Note: These issues take a long time to resolve. The last grievance appeal meeting occurred a few weeks ago, more than two years after the original incident. I believe this case will be resolved without going to arbitration, as I believe we are going to make an offer to reduce the suspension to three days.

D.J., when I read this, I was glad to see you had clearly understood what I meant by internal conflict. It has nothing to do with either the two technicians or your senior management team. It is all about *you* and the struggle you experienced between being the kind of manager you want to be and being the type of team player you want be. You just happen to be caught in the middle between yourselves.

All quality help or therapy shifts your awareness to a higher level. Internal conflict is resolved at a level above where it is created. Sometimes a good friend can help another by listening and asking questions. The only way to resolve internal conflict is to go up a level, which may mean reorganization. So what does going up a level sound like? Here's an example from my experience. I have for about three years now been in conflict about being the teacher I want to be and the employee I want to be, both higher level references. The teacher I want to be is one who teaches to the best of my ability the information I believe to be the most current and technically correct. The type of employee I want to be is one who fulfills my contract and goes above and beyond to meet the expectations of my employer. At times, I have been asked to teach content that I do not

believe is accurate. One day I sat down with Tim Carey, a friend and therapist, to discuss this internal conflict. After about twenty minutes of him helping me explore my background thoughts, a phrase popped into my head: "Be passionate about what you know." Somehow I knew that if I could hang onto that idea over time, I would reorganize and resolve the conflict. At that moment, I couldn't have told you what I might do or how I might do it, but I knew that I had bumped it up!

Resolving conflict may require a major overhaul or rewiring of the system. In PCT terms, we call this reorganization. It is this process that Plooij and Vanderijt describe as developmental leaps in babies. Even as adults, reorganization is one way in which we learn and gain new abilities and skills. Internal conflict holds the gift of growth.

Bump it up and let it go!

In a nutshell

- 🐚 PCT describes internal conflict as the inability for the system to create two different references at the same level at the same time.

- 🐚 Internal conflict isn't about anyone or anything else but me; it's not a matter of right or wrong.

- 🐚 Internal conflict involves three levels of perception: the level at which it plays out, the level at which it is created, and the level at which it can be resolved.

- 🐚 Internal conflict can only be resolved by going up a level and may involve reorganizing.

- 🐚 Resolving high level internal conflict almost always requires the help of an outsider.

CHAPTER 11

Dear Tomas,

Change and Perceptual Control Theory

*W*hen I first met Tomas, we instantly connected. We share a love of adventure and a passion for travel and people. In an instant, we can go from having a philosophical discussion to singing a song from our teenage years in two-part harmony.

At the time of our meeting, Tomas was absorbed in his career in the human resources department of a major medical conglomerate. He worked eighty-hour weeks and felt personally connected to most of the people he came in contact with. Tomas was born in Puerto Rico and grew up in New York City. Because of his inability to speak English when he moved to New York as a child, he felt isolated in school and was in a special class for retarded children. This experience contributed to his desire to become multi-lingual. Tomas is now fluent in five languages. During his world travels, his ability to speak multiple languages has come in handy.

During the time we have known each other, Tomas received his personal coaching license. He has a strong drive to help others become the best they can be, according to their own standards. His job, as well as his nature, is to help people thrive even in the midst of chaos. It is his life-long official and unofficial role in helping others as they go through change that serves as the basis for this letter.

Dear Tomas,

*T*oday, I was sitting here at my desk, thinking about change. You and I have made careers out of helping others with the change process. It always amazes me that every time we think we have a handle on life, we turn around and something is different. I'm glad that when I was younger I had a good support system and that I had opportunities to experience change and learn how to be more successful at handling it. I'd like to start with some personal reflections about change, talk a bit about the bigger context of systems thinking and then about personal and organizational change in the context of Perceptual Control Theory.

When I was in eighth grade I woke one morning to find my whole world was changing. Or at least that is what I thought when I found out we were moving out of the only house I had ever known and going half-way across the country to California and my brother wasn't moving with us. I was leaving behind cold winters with white Christmases and gaining a pool in the back yard. I had ridden a bus every day of my school life, and now I would be walking to school. At that moment, I learned one of the most important lessons about change: that I am not in control of my environment. I cannot plan or predict what is going to come next. This is a lesson that can be scary, and learning how to ride with it is one of life's big challenges. Recently my older son Wesley moved back home four years after he completed high school. I think he keeps expecting to wake up one morning and have an epiphany and know exactly what he wants to do for the rest of his life. I keep reminding him that "understanding" usually doesn't happen that way, and that even when we think we've decided on a direction to take our lives, life has a way of taking us down a totally different path. Don't get me wrong: it isn't that he shouldn't prepare for a career. He actually needs to prepare for what I think of as a fluid career, one that can take many paths.

My grandmother was born in 1900. Being born at the turn of a century seems a bit mystical. When she was a child, the major modes of transportation involved walking or using a horse. She was a first generation American and was born on a small farm in South Dakota. She was a gutsy lady; before she turned 20, she and her sister traveled half way across the country from the farm to Oregon in a Model T. For her time, that was an almost unheard of adventure. Before she died, men had landed on the moon, and the Concord was in use for commercial air travel. I always admired her ability to deal with change, but now I realize that the amount of change she had experienced in eighty-plus years, I probably experience in ten years or less. When I think about how many changes will occur for my sons in their lifetimes, I'm stupefied. Just the other night, I was talking with my younger son about a time when I couldn't look up something on the Internet, and I realized that my sons have never lived without the Internet. They haven't known a time when phones were not cordless, and, perish the thought, when TVs didn't have color. Change is the foundation of today's culture. Learning to handle change and to self-evaluate are, I think, at the heart of taking more effective control of our lives.

Tomas, both of our careers involve helping people and organizations handle change. A key thought that helps me is that change happens without our consent, in very unexpected ways. I know that during times of change, I am going to feel a strong desire to control things because everything seems out of my control. What I've realized is that my job is to figure out how to move through change with patience and perseverance so that I come out of the process renewed. This is not an easy task.

Rosabeth Moss Kantor, an authority on organizational change, uses a phrase that I think describes both of us: change masters. In the past three years, you've lived in Minnesota, Puerto Rico, and New York City. You've gone from working eighty-hour weeks, to walking the beach, to starting your own business, to working in a medical human resources department, to being laid off. Through it all, I have heard about the excitement and sense of adventure each change and new challenge has brought you. Kantor describes change masters as "those people and organizations adept at the art of anticipating the need for change, and of leading productive change." I believe it is this attitude of embracing change and seeing it as an opportunity that has helped you feel more in control of your life.

We see change in much the same way as the Chinese, whose written language expresses thoughts and ideas through the use of symbols. The Chinese use two symbols to represent both *change* and *crisis*. The symbol on the left is the symbol for *danger*, and the one on the right is the symbol for *opporutnity*.

危 機

Pronunciation: *wei jee*

These symbols capture the idea that change, although painful, is a natural process, and that when it is viewed as an opportunity for growth, change can be less stressful.

As a human resources director, you have helped people change how they operate on the job, assisted in hiring people new to a profession, helped foreign-born workers bridge cultural differences, and laid people off. Your whole job has been about change and helping others through the process. For ten years, my job was to use research to facilitate change in schools. I worked with improvement teams that were helping others build capacity for organizational and personal change. One thing I think both of us realized early in our careers is that change and transition are individual processes and happen one person at a time. But there are ways to facilitate these processes, to speed them up. There are also ways to facilitate large-scale change in organizations, as long as we don't lose sight of the individuals along the way.

Before we go further with this topic, I want to talk about the concept of systems thinking. I have talked about the importance of getting out of 'box and label' thinking and not thinking in terms of linear models like stimulus-response. I've invited you to think about circular causation, nested hierarchies, and negative feedback loops. But I haven't backed up and painted the big picture of systems thinking. Now we need to examine the energy around us, the air we've been breathing, and bring some ideas together. It is important to remember that learning happens first through experiencing and second through categorizing. That's the way the levels of perception are developed, so we might as well take advantage of our natural learning process that builds from the lower levels to the higher levels.

Thinking in terms of linear causation, simply boxing and labeling, fragments the world and limits what we see.

To better understand this, imagine walking down the street. First, walk a short distance watching only your feet. Next, look at the ground a few feet ahead of you. Finally, raise your eyes and look to the horizon. What's the same and what's different in each experience? Were you amazed at how much more you saw and noticed when you looked to the horizon? When we look to the horizon, we often have the impression we are "seeing it all," especially if we are standing on the shore overlooking a large body of water. Then we realize that we don't see what's immediately behind us, so we turn around. Does this give us the whole picture? Can we see it all? If we believe only what we see, we would believe the world is flat. We might think that if we walk too far, we'll fall off the edge. Next, we would act in certain ways based on this belief. That's because when we think in parts — such as focusing only on what we can see — we miss the whole. When we look to the horizon and get a bigger picture, we need to remember that we are still seeing only part of the earth and there is a whole lot more we need to understand. We need to have faith in what we cannot see from where we are standing. This is part of systems thinking, realizing we can't see it all at once and that talking and thinking about the parts doesn't give us the whole picture. Fritjof Capra says in *The Web of Life*, "Nature is but a moving order, a pattern of relationships within an organized whole."

To understand systems thinking we need to first understand what a system is. Look around you, make a mental list of what you believe are systems and what you believe are not. For a moment, I want you to think in terms of boxes and labels. I've provided you with a table in which you can record some of your thinking. Check out your list with a friend. See if you can put at least five things in each category.

System	Not a System

Is there a characteristic that all of the things you listed under system have in common? What about all of the things you have listed under not a system? Where would you put a car? Where would you put a tree? How about a computer? How about a rock? How about a pencil? What about gasoline?

According to Andrea Shapiro in *Creating Contagious Commitment,* "A system is a collection of components that interact together to function as a whole." Linda Booth Sweeney in *When a Butterfly Sneezes* suggests five critical attributes of a system:

1 Things change if you take away one of the parts.

2 It's collectively more than the sum of its parts; there are a huge number of tightly connected interactions. Remember that relationships are critical in systems.

3 It has a distinct point or purpose in relationship to a larger system in which it is embedded. Many systems are made up of multiple sub-systems, like your own body.

4 Its causes are circular, not linear. One event causes another event, and that second event comes back around to influence the first event. For example, assuming a stable environment, more births lead to a larger population, a larger population leads to more potential parents. This leads to more births, which leads to a larger population, and a larger population leads to more possible parents, and on and on.

5 Systems have a tendency to repeat patterns in different contexts. Sometimes these patterns are called systems archetypes. Gas price wars would be an example of one archetype, where gas station *A* decreases the price, so gas station *B* decreases the price to remain competitive. Gas station *A* decreases its price again, and so on. We are back to circles again. This pattern is what many think of as friendly competition. But where does it get us?

Now go back to your list and see how you did. Do the things you have listed under *system* fit the description? Many *living things* or collections of living things fit under the system category. For example, let's look at a lake as a system. (1) A lake is a collection of fish, plants, water, rocks, sand and so on. Take away one of the parts and things change. (2) If I only showed you a fish, would you understand what a lake was? If you knew everything there was to know about sand, would you understand a lake? Each part has its own function in relation to the whole. (3) The purpose a lake serves is only one part of the larger ecosystem in which it exists. It both contributes to the system and takes away from the system. Think about the water cycle: evaporation, transpiration, condensation, precipitation, and runoff. The lake is only one component of a larger system. (4) Small fish feed off of the available plant life in the lake, the larger fish (predators) eat the smaller fish, the predator fish defecate, fertilizing the plants, which creates healthy plant growth, which supports the small fish, which support the bigger fish, and so on.

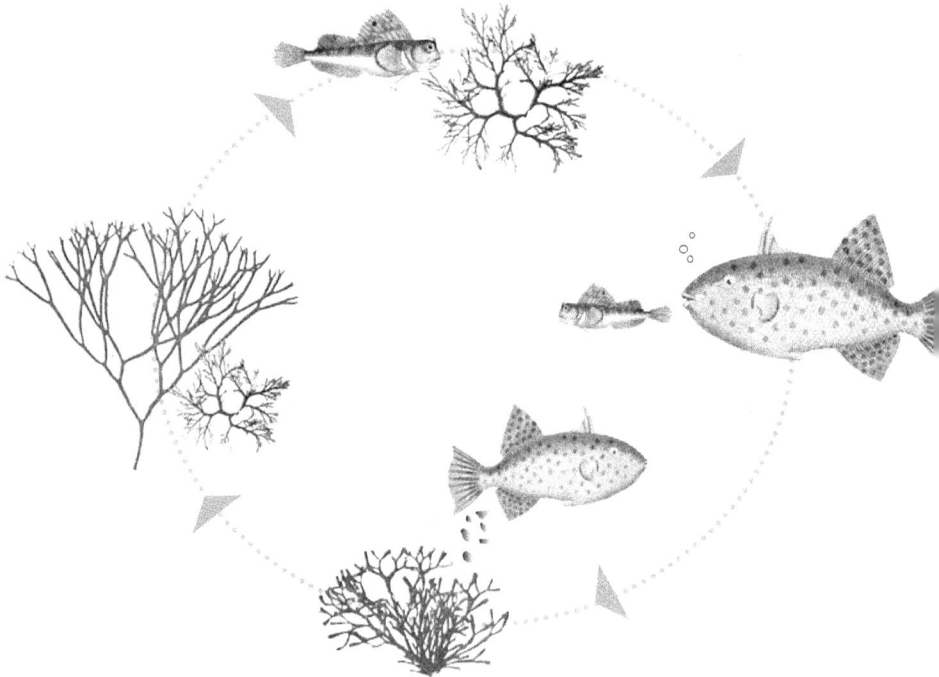

(5) Let's look at one systems archetype that applies to a lake system: *Fixes that Fail.* In a lake, when fishing begins to decline, the lake is often stocked with fish from a hatchery. The belief is that adding fish will improve sport fishing. In the short term, this is true. However, in the long run, the stocked fish eat too many of the minnows, and the fish population can actually decrease faster than it would have if left alone. Sometimes a quick fix results in a long-term problem of greater magnitude.

Once we know we are looking at a system, there are three things that are essential to becoming a systems thinker:

1 Looking at the relationships among the parts; seeing the whole.

2 Understanding the effects of time.

3 Understanding the system's feedback loops.

I call these the big three of systems thinking: relationships, context, and connectedness. Systems thinkers examine the relationships among the parts and the role of each part in the bigger system, they look for connections in circles and they understand that each system is unique to its context. Let's look at a lake system to better understand context. Most lakes in Minnesota and Wisconsin have sandy bottoms, and are clear enough to see the bottom several feet deep because they were formed by glaciers. But lakes in other parts of the country may have rock or clay bottoms; some have virtually no visibility once the water is more than a few inches deep. Those lakes exist in different contexts.

What we experience of a system is its dynamics, the interactions between the components of the system. Some dynamics in the lake are the growth of plants or the laying of eggs on the fish beds. Some dynamics in a work setting could be conversations of people during the change process. In a system, the interaction of the components are always affected by time. Some of these interactions appear to happen almost instantaneously. For others, it may take years to see the full effects of the dynamics within the system. Something that happens to a person in childhood may seem insignificant at the time, but it may have a long-term impact on the person's life. An example from your childhood was not speaking English when you moved from Puerto Rico to New York. It is only now, as you look back, that you realize how small circumstances can have great effects. Recently, I went to see the movie *Take the Lead* in which the main character, played by Antonio Banderas, portrays ballroom dancer Pierre Dulaine. The film revolves around a group of high school detention students in the New York City public school system, where Dulaine volunteers to teach. One of my favorite lines is when he tells the students that although others may see them as failures, all he sees when he looks at them are choices. A systems thinker understands how small choices can make big differences. Context does not completely define the system — we are not our circumstances — but our circumstances play a role in *who we become.*

Most often systems thinkers see the interrelationships in a system in terms of the effects of time and describe them as feedback loops. There are two basic types of feedback loops, reinforcing loops and balancing loops. They sometimes are called by different names, like augmenting loops and negative feedback loops. What you already know about the *loop* will come into play in this bigger discussion of systems. So this is a great example of nesting ideas. I like to think of reinforcing loops or augmenting loops in terms of managing money. Compounding interest is an example of a reinforcing loop. If you are saving money, the more you save, the greater the amount of interest you earn, which increases your balance, which increases your amount of earned interest. If you are paying a loan, compounding means you will owe more because very little goes to paying off the principle of the loan. This is what makes a loan-shark rich. Over time, reinforcing loops either get larger and larger or smaller and smaller. Since living systems cannot continue to grow or continue to shrink and still survive, you don't often see long-term examples of these types of loops in nature. Extinction of a species would be one example of a reinforcing loop. Saving the condors in California is an excellent example of systems thinking. Environmentalists are paying attention to not only the bird's birth cycles but also the context (habitat) and the relationship of the birds to each other, the environment, and other factors.

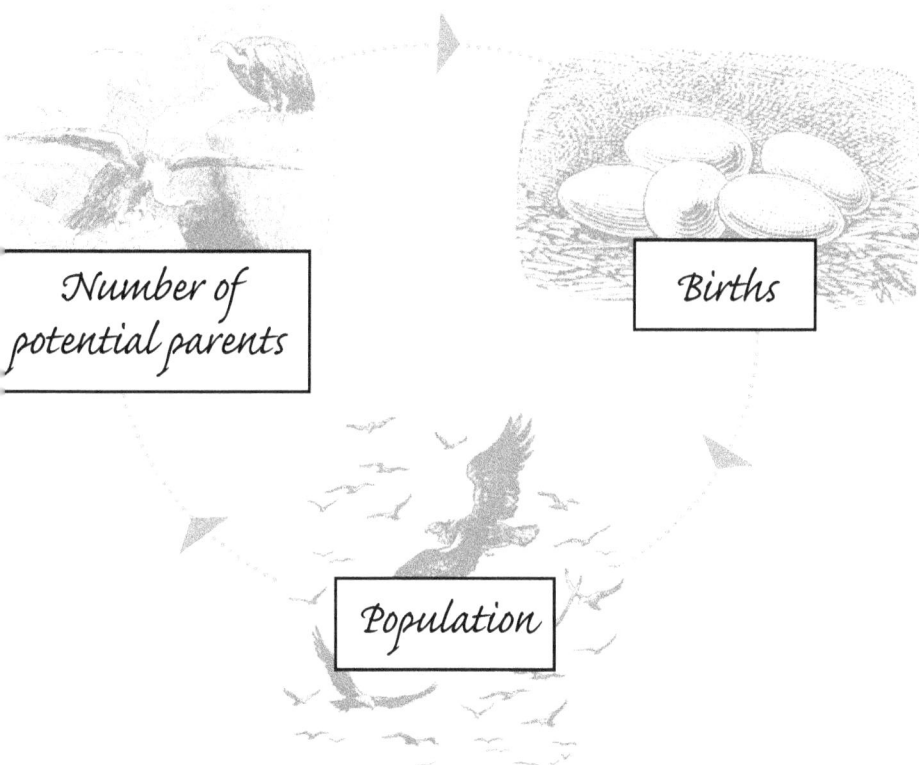

Number of potential parents

Births

Population

Take a look at this example. If the number of births goes up, what happens? If the number of births goes down what happens? What if thousands of people move into the area? What if the local water supply is contaminated by bio-terrorism? This is a reinforcing or augmenting loop, and whatever direction it starts moving, it will continue in that direction unless other checks and balances act upon it.

Condor populations began declining, and that trend continued until man purposefully intervened to save the species.
Without intervention, the system, in this case the species,
disappears. Time is critical because the change depends on
how quickly the loop is reinforcing and the delay between
the components of the loop. These types of loops are never
stable and are not goal oriented. But in the change process,
they can come in handy.

By contrast, balancing loops or negative feedback loops
are designed to *maintain a specific goal.* An example is the
new digital temperature control device in cars. You set the
system for a specific temperature, and the system then turns
on and off and selects heating or cooling depending on what
temperature is being registered in the car at the time. In
balancing loops, the system has a tendency to oscillate depending on the delay (the time it takes for the components to
act to counter the difference between the present state and
the goal). The longer the delay the slower the oscillation. The
oscillation is limited by the capacity of the system to change
and act. Remember that the negative feedback loop is one
of the basic concepts in PCT. In the Powers model, the time
delay is built into the functions. When changes are required
at the higher levels (programs, principles, system concepts)
there will in all likelihood be slower oscillation (wavering).
Why? Because these loops operate more slowly; it takes
them longer to counter disturbances because more lower
level loops are involved the higher you go up the levels of
perception. This slow oscillation may make it difficult to observe changes in a person's behavior. At lower levels, oscillation occurs faster. Think about a muscle twitch, a low-level
action. The speed at which the twitching occurs is faster
than, say, your action, perhaps your over-steering a car.

Reinforcing loops drive the system away from a steady
state and toward growth or decline. Balancing loops try to

put the system into a steady state. What are some examples of the two types of loops from your experiences? Think about a group of people, like members of a classroom, or a gang, or a division in a large company. Describe the relationship among the parts. How might time affect these systems? Can you think of some examples of both balancing and reinforcing loops that play out in each group? Ask a friend, especially someone familiar with the same group, what he thinks. Or think about what has happened with a major sports team over time as players are traded, coaches come and go, or new regulations affect the game.

I have always been a believer in the benefits of people working together. I believe diversity among group members is a great strength. That's probably a result of having gone to a high school with students from fifty different countries. Throughout my lifetime, I have liked belonging to groups. I've helped start a local sorority, Phi Epsilon Alpha, at St. Cloud State University, and an international organization, IAACT, the International Association for the Application of Control Theory. In both of these cases, the groups formed when problems at the principles level in the parent organizations grew over time. Issues that presented small problems to a parent group kept growing until the group could no longer tolerate the stresses. A subgroup broke off, and a new entity was created. Based on what you've learned or already know about systems thinking, how would you describe what happened in terms of loops, relationships, and context?

In another group to which I belonged, we had a wide variety of people with a wide variety of opinions and styles. Somehow, even though we had many heated arguments, in the end we came to appreciate the diversity of the group. We realized the customers that members of the group each wanted to serve would benefit from the variety of opinions within our group. We came to value the group diversity because our goal was clear, we all agreed on the goal and its value, and we each achieved our individual purposes by reaching the goal. What type of loop does this group process represent?

In the business world, these ideas have translated quite easily into the language of organizational change, but one vital element has been left out. The missing key factor is *people* and their behavior. Every author I've read who has written about change — Margaret Wheatly, Peter Senge, Marvin Weisbord, Andrea Shapiro, and others — embraces systems thinking until the author considers the individual. At that point in the discussion, people are put into boxes, and each box is given a label: apathetics, incubators, advocates, resisters, innovators, early adopters, early majority, late majority, laggards, originators, pragmatists, conservers, mavens, connectors, and salesmen. Change masters are encouraged to remember what criteria places a person into a particular box, what the label is, and how to deal with each of the different sub-groups.

This is where PCT comes in. To put it simply, when we are trying to change an organization, we want to create a reinforcing loop for the "new" in terms of the system as a whole and realize that each person is operating as a balancing loop. We need to pay attention to the content, context, and carriers.

For an organization to change, the people in it must have a personal reference of the desire for the "new." All individuals must see how the "new" will help them get what they want. Some refer to this as a link to a high profile need. The linking is done by connecting, connecting, connecting, not by boxing and labeling. The fastest way to connect is to *listen* with a new set of ears. This new set of ears comes from understanding behavior in a PCT context. We must listen for the *references* of the individual, listen for the *error*, and help the person see how the change will help to reduce their own individual error. We need to find out what's not working for all individuals and see if the "new" will get them more of what they want. It is important to listen *at the highest level possible.* If an individual is talking about doing things in a different order or sequence, talk with them about the program. If they are talking about the program, help them understand the principles that support the program. If they are talking about the principles they want to live by, talk with them about their mental models and how they believe the world operates. Keep bumping it up! Understand that much of what is happening in the change process is disturbance and that some disturbances will be facilitating forces and others will be hindering forces. Always remember that each individual will always have unique internal standards.

Bump up your listening

- *Reference*
- *Error*
- *Highest level*

On the larger systems scale, look for patterns in the organization and try to describe them in terms of loops. Then create a reinforcing loop that moves the organization in the direction of the desired change. This is done by making sure that people understand the content of the change. You want to create a contagious context and model principles of PCT with the carriers, those committed to facilitating change. Typically, large-scale change efforts have a pattern of acceptance and support. The trick is to figure out how to keep the energy moving towards acceptance and support and to avoid negativity. You can keep the energy moving toward acceptance and support by building networks within networks. Typically, people think of building a network one individual at a time along the lines of building a pyramid. Start with one person, add two more, then add three, and so on. I prefer to think of network building in terms of a sequence in nature that appears everywhere you look, known as the Fibonacci sequence. In nature, items such as shells, plants, crystals, and pinecones exhibit natural growth that builds in a sequence: 0, 1, 1, 2, 3, 5, 8, 13, 21, 24, 55, 89, 144, 233, 377, 610, 987... The sequence is created using addition, $0+1=1$, $1+1=2$, $1+2=3$. Each number in the sequence is added to the one before it to find the next number. I like to think of building networks within networks as following a similar natural sequence. When you initiate change, often there are no initial supporters, but if you can tap into what people want and how change can help them, soon you'll have a carrier to help facilitate the change, and then another, and the network begins to grow exponentially.

All individuals in the organization need to be involved in some way. The involvement may be as simple as being informed of the changes. Most importantly, you want information to flow from inside the system, and that's where carriers come in. Carriers are the subgroup of people who quickly commit to facilitating the change. Like the allies of World War II, they may represent many different cultures and subgroups. In fact, they should be a diverse group, and management may need to purposefully recruit carriers. They have a collective mission to see the change through.

Carriers need to be provided with continual formal and informal opportunities to learn about and discuss the change. One indicator of a healthy organization is that individuals in the group feel comfortable, especially during the change process, expressing feelings that may appear to be polar opposites, like excitement and fear, or joy and sadness. Think of any major event in your life, and I would guess you had polar opposite feelings. Typically, one of these is "politically correct" and the other isn't. In the natural, healthy process of change, many people experience this same phenomenon, and it needs to be OK for them to express it. (A word of caution here: there is a difference between expressing it and wallowing in it.)

Effective change carriers also model the change and tap into their previously established social and professional networks, which may be one-to-one or one-to-many, spontaneous or planned. It only takes close proximity for germs to spread. Carriers and their networks are often the best defense for preventing problems before they arise. Management needs to listen carefully when the carriers point out road blocks, pot holes, and detours. Although not everyone in the organization will be a carrier, thinking of everyone as cooperating will help you operate from the principles level. After all, each individual has a unique way of cooperating. The change master's job is to figure out how to tap into it.

Systems change requires attention to everyone in the organization, the nurturing of the carriers, and a context that supports the change. To borrow from the medical model we can think of the context as needing to be contagious. As with the common cold, change can spread very quickly with little effort on the carriers' part in the right context. For management, it's a matter of making sure that those who are "contagious" have maximum contact with each other and as many people in the system as possible. Look again to nature, and ask yourself how you can build networks within networks of individuals in the system. What are the ideal conditions for spreading the change?

In general the context must be one where it is OK to make a mistake. There will be oscillation in behavior. Remember the old saying "two steps forward and one step back." In a contagious context, there are group celebrations of successes, not continual individual recognition.

Rosabeth Moss Kantor in *The Change Masters* writes, "Hope of obtaining conventional rewards seems to play very little role in stimulating innovativeness." When organizations, families, or groups of any kind build in reward systems, they also build in punishment systems. Rewards and punishments are flip sides of the same coin. Such systems end up with haves and have nots, and this seldom leads to cooperation, growth, and support. It is impossible to reward some people without giving others the feeling that they have been punished. Also, what one person considers a reward another may not. To test this idea yourself, come up with a list of five ways to reward yourself, and then go to someone you don't know very well, and ask that person to do the same. Compare your lists.

In addition to being a context of celebration, communication, and dialog, contagious environments also provide constant access to information and the infrastructure necessary to support change. It is virtually impossible to provide too much access to information. The key word here is "access." Each person needs to know where and how to get the information she wants. There is an expression in education that applies: just because you taught it doesn't mean they learned it. If you give people an answer before they have a question, they may not recognize its importance or usefulness. They might not even hear it.

The contagious context must be free of germicides! This means that competing pressures need to be removed so there is a clear message of what is significant. Besides the importance of being clear that the "new" is a priority, there needs to be some discussion about what accepted evidence of movement looks like and sounds like. I usually ask those who are involved in a change, "What will we accept as evidence of results?" "How will we know we are getting what we want?" When those involved are clear on what to look and listen for, change will have a greater chance of happening. That's because the group will be controlling for specific reference perceptions.

Some parts of the infrastructure are specific to the content of the change effort. For example, if an expectation is for employees to travel less and telecommute more, everyone needs to have access to technology and be trained in how to use it. A change master asks "What are the resources and knowledge that individuals will need to be successful with the 'new'?"

Remember that people experiencing change feel a loss of control. An effective infrastructure helps minimize those feelings by being aware of the losses individuals may fear most and creating a context to assist individuals through their individual losses. Here are a few ways in which folks typically feel they may lose during change.

✳ Economic loss
✳ Loss of status, importance, and influence
✳ Loss of professional creativity
✳ Turf loss (physical space, expertise-based responsibility, or organizational power)
✳ Loss of attachments (peer relationships, mentorships, collegial trust, group membership)
✳ Loss of structure (time schedules, routine responsibilities, familiar procedures, and priorities)

* Loss of meaning (the purpose of things, the "why," the reason one does what one does)
* Future loss (dreams, expectations of and plans for one's personal and professional future)

In addition to anticipating perceived losses, the context needs to support renorming. The work of William Bridges refers to this as *transitions*, the psychological renorming that occurs after change, what I think of as the recovery factor, and what in PCT we might call the process of reorganization. This is a natural process that involves letting go of an old situation, suffering through a period of confusion, and experiencing a time of reorientation and recovery. In PCT, we say that the confusion period is characterized by the system appearing to be out of control, trying random actions to counter disturbance and reduce the large amount of error it is experiencing. If you have ever seen a chicken getting its head cut off, you know exactly what this looks like. Frans Plooij and Hetty Vanderijt talk about regression-conflict-jump. I like this idea because it suggests that the path of learning is never smooth, straight, or easy. Recently, my son Wesley drove from Minnesota to Georgia. I talked with him about six hours into the drive, and he said to me, "They need to put some curves or hills or something on these roads; this is soooo boring!" Change is rarely as boring as the freeways of the Midwest; change is full of curves, hills, and lots of variety. So give yourself a break, expect some detours, and enjoy the scenery along the road to change.

I've mentioned that change in organizations follows a pattern of acceptance and support. Before I got involved with PCT, I often used the analogy of the transformation of a caterpillar into a butterfly to describe the process an individual or an organization goes through after change occurs. The message was that change happens outside of us, that we go through internal changes only after experiencing the external change, and that the internal change takes time. I've since altered the analogy. In PCT, we call a major internal change *reorganization*. The internal process has three overlapping phases: the caterpillar stage of letting go, the cocoon stage of the neutral zone, and the butterfly stage of emerging renewal. Although many researchers describe these three basic phases, they also acknowledge that change is a uniquely individualized process. This is where, as a systems thinker, paying attention to time is helpful. As a change master, when I'm dealing with personal change, I need to remember to give myself and others time to work through the process. We need time to wallow a bit and be OK with not having all the answers, trusting that our systems will figure things out. We need to remember that we have the answers within us. That is how we were designed. Humans are some of the most adaptable creatures on Earth. We need to remember this in the midst of the chaos.

It is important to remember what you already understand about the levels of perception, particularly that the higher levels set references for lower levels, and that the higher you go, the slower the process. You must also remember that conflict is only resolved at a level above where it was created. So the higher the change, the longer it may take for the system to reorganize. Changing principles takes longer than changing the sequence in which we do something. Take a moment and think about changing your morning routine. Here's an example. I recently moved my undies to a different drawer in my dresser. Keep in mind they have been in the same drawer for about twenty-five years. For the first week, I kept going to the old drawer every morning. The next week I got a little better in remembering to go to the "new" drawer, and I got better and better as the weeks passed. But still, five months later, I occasionally find myself going to the old drawer. Creating a new sequence isn't easy. It takes time! And I *wanted* the undie drawer change. Now imagine how difficult it might be to make a change at a higher level. What happens to the time frame if we're pushed into a change we don't want?

In *Living Control Systems*, Phil Runkel quotes Powers as saying, "No system ever changes itself... In PCT, there is no such thing as a 'self-organizing system.' If change occurs, we have to consider both the system that is changed and the system that is responsible for making the changes."

What does this mean for you and me? First, PCT supports the idea that change occurs from the outside. In PCT, a change outside of the system (in this case "system" could mean a specific loop) manifests in massive internal error, that the present hierarchy can no longer control to reduce the error. The reorganizing system is activated, and the system begins to randomly attempt actions to gain control. PCT supports the idea that change takes time, and *always* involves error. In fact there is a direct link: as the rate of error increases, the rate of reorganization increases.

While the reorganizing system is taking random actions, trying to find one or more actions that singly or in concert will reduce error, the system is stressed. To re-establish control, two contextual features after change are paramount: modeling of new behaviors and understanding that it is OK to make a mistake. Think back to Plooij and Vanderijt's discussion of baby development. How do babies learn and change so much in the first months after birth? They are surrounded by models of how to behave, and those around them accept that they are going to make mistakes.

A third feature to creating a reinforcing loop for change is making sure that everyone understands the content of the change — and I mean *everyone* who will be involved in the process! At the very least, everyone in the organization needs to be informed that a change is taking place and needs to know what that change is. The more someone is expected to change, the more relevance they must find in the content of the change. The necessary information may be provided to individuals or subgroups. Insure that everyone has access to information at all times. The last thing you want to do is say something like, "I already told you that," or "Didn't you get the memo?" Remember, just because you taught it doesn't mean they learned it.

Relationships among professionals within an organizations range from vigorously healthy to dangerously competitive. Strengthen those relationships, and you improve professional practice and create support for change. The fastest way to pass on the basic content of any change effort is to provide large scale, large group overviews. However, a deeper understanding requires a form of professional facilitation that is quite different from the workshop-driven approach. Organizations that have developed learning communities to initiate changes are usually more successful in supporting implementation. The most powerful forms of learning occur in teams that meet on a regular basis for the purposes of learning, joint planning, and problem solving. These teams, often called learning communities or communities of practice, operate with a commitment to the norms of continuous improvement and experimentation and engage the members in improving their daily work to advance the goals of the entire organization.

Here's a chart with a few key points about the carriers, context, and content of change. Posting it can act as a daily reminder of what we've talked about.

Change Through a Systems Lens

Carriers

* Build networks within networks, both formal and informal.

* Champion training beyond the content of the "new." Focus on communication skills, the change process, and systems thinking.

* Replicate demographics of the organization. Subgroups should consist of the same demographics as the organization as a whole. Take into account gender, ethnicity, representation of management, laborers, and so on.

* Think of building networks in terms of the Fibonacci sequence, using natural progression and growth patterns.

Context

* Champion the ideal that it's OK to make a mistake.
* Minimize the categories of loss.
* Provide all necessary resources.
* Provide adequate time for renorming and acquiring new skills.

Content

* Impart information to everyone through large scale overviews.

* Create and maintain learning communities for deep learning and supporting change.

* Connect content to individual reference perceptions; keep it relevant.

* Create dialog across divisions and sub-groups.

To effectively facilitate large-scale change, it is benefi cial to create learning communities or support groups that cut across typical division lines. A change master must pay close attention to the bigger picture and the relationships among the parts. The change process may fail if attention is not given to the interconnectedness across subgroups or divisions.

Those who are going to act as the carriers of change will be more successful and feel more supported if their knowledge goes beyond understanding the "new" and includes knowledge of effective communication (*listening*), systems thinking, and the change process. In addition, those in leadership or management roles need to understand all of these things and act as champions and forerunners by modeling the "new." This is especially important if the change involves altering the organization's culture or some of its long-held practices.

The bottom line in the whole process is that change is about the individual. When you are in the midst of change, *you need to be your own change agent.*

1 View change as an opportunity for growth.

2 Create a support network, and don't be afraid to ask for help.

3 Ask yourself what losses are you perceiving and how might you overcome them. Remember that to grab onto something new, you often must let go of something you are holding on to.

4 Remember that it's OK to make a mistake.

5 Give yourself time!

6 Think about your relationships and connections.

7 Be aware of the context in which you exist.

8 Think like a systems thinker; think of feedback loops, time, and the whole.

9 Remember what you've learned about the change process:

- You will probably feel out of control.

- Change is a winding path of growth.

- You may experience opposing feelings like sadness and joy.

- Humans are extremely adaptable creatures.

- You will eventually figure it out because that's how we stay alive.

10 Celebrate your small successes!

One of the most important things I've learned about change in my life is that it isn't going away any time soon. I might as well learn from each experience, and that knowledge will help with the next change. One practice I've found valuable is to give myself credit for what I have accomplished each day. We are designed to see what's not working, so especially during the change process we need to purposefully focus on what is working. When I learned to water ski, I didn't make it up or around the whole lake the first time, but I kept at it, and each time, my skiing got a little better. I made a mental list every time of how it took less tries to get up or how much farther around the lake I made it. Change is like that for me now. I don't always like it, and I don't want to fall. But each time I've gone through change, I've learned more about myself, and I've gotten better at handling it. Most importantly, it has helped me grow as a person.

Recently, my son Duncan was online looking into the armed forces, and he found this saying on the U.S. Marine's web site, "Pain is weakness leaving the body." If change is always painful (filled with error), then with each passing change, I can only be getting stronger!

May life present you with many dangerous opportunities.

In a nutshell

🐚 Change happens outside of the system.

🐚 Reorganization and gaining the ability to control new variables (learning) happens within the system.

🐚 Although a natural process, change always involves pain and error.

🐚 Learning to handle change and learning self-evaluation skills are at the heart of taking more effective control of our lives.

🐚 What we experience is the interaction of a system's parts.

🐚 There are two types of feedback loops, reinforcing and balancing loops.

🐚 Reinforcing loops drive the system away from a steady state, toward growth or decline. Balancing loops (or negative feedback loops) try to put the system into a steady state.

🐚 Systems thinkers think in terms of feedback loops, time, and the whole.

🐚 Systems thinkers ask themselves questions about context, connectedness, and relationships.

🜚 When we want groups to change, we need to build reinforcing loops that support the change.

🜚 We need to remember that people change, not the system, and that people operate based on negative feedback or balancing loops.

🜚 The higher up the levels of perception the change is, the longer it will take to implement.

🜚 Act as your own *change master*. Ask yourself:

　🜚 What are the resources and knowledge necessary to be successful with the "new"? How can I get these?

　🜚 What losses might I experience and how might I overcome these or protect myself? What can I let go of?

　🜚 Have I given myself and others time to adjust to the change?

　🜚 What networks do I have to support me through the process?

　🜚 Who do I want to be when I feel out of control?

　🜚 How am I spending my time and energy? Am I fighting the change or trying to figure it out?

　🜚 Have I given myself credit for what I've accomplished?

CHAPTER 12

Dear Sandy,

Reorganization

and

learning

When I worked for the state department of education in Minnesota, I was afforded the exciting opportunity to be involved in cutting edge research on change and effective school practices. I met, worked along side of, and learned from some of the country's top educational leaders. My role involved helping school leadership teams facilitate change.

During this time, I met Sandy, who was principal of an elementary school with more than six hundred students. Sandy took a traditional K-6 elementary school and, as she says, changed the wheels on the plane while it was flying. It became a school that did not label students as learning disabled, gifted and talented, behavioral disordered, or any of the alphabet soup the educational system often applies to learners. It became a school in which competency and skill were used to determine how students were grouped for each major unit of study. It became a school in which instruction was built around technology, cooperative group learning, and multi-age grouping.

While working on her doctorate, Sandy had done extensive research on leadership and its relation to change. She was especially interested in uncovering the critical characteristics that an individual needs to become a transformational leader.

Sandy has been over the years a supporter of working within the system and in the best interest of the students. She and I have had many strategy sessions on helping school administrators, state departments of education, and managers champion change in systems. These discussions are the foundation for this letter.

Dear Sandy,

Learning is such a huge topic and one you and I have discussed many times. One day you asked me, "How does your understanding of Perceptual Control Theory help you better understand teaching and learning?" I've thought about that a lot. Here's the short answer: the three key elements in PCT that have most helped me understand teaching and learning are (1) how memory fits into the PCT model, (2) how the hierarchy works, and (3) how we *reorganize*.

Think about what the word *learning* means to you. What is your personal definition? Check out the answer with a few other folks. Is learning being able to repeat what the teacher said? Is learning as simple as gaining knowledge? Does it require the ability to apply that new knowledge? Is learning being able to apply what you have learned in new and different settings? Is memorizing a list of facts learning? Think of the last thing you learned. What was it and how did you learn it? Did it require a teacher? Is learning fun? Is learning painful? What role does memory play?

Think about how different types of learning take place. Memorizing a rule (*I* before *E* except after *C* or when sounded like *A* as in *neighbor* and *weigh*) is different from learning to ride a bicycle. Thus they require different types of teaching. Bill Powers in *Behavior: The Control of Perception* lists three types of learning: memory, problem-solving programs, and reorganization. Let's take a look at these in some depth.

First, let's turn to the loop diagram that shows the flow of information in a living system and add one more component, memory. Powers defines memory as the storage and retrieval of information carried by neural signals. Powers goes on to describe memory as having a third feature: selection. You can think of memory like a music recording system, where the recording, playback, and selection functions are all important.

Think of how our music memories have been stored over our lifetimes. When we were young, we used vinyl records. Then eight-track cartridge tapes became available. Next, we switched to cassette-tape recording. Now we have new choices: you have your music on CDs and my kids store theirs as MP3 files on their iPods. Each device has a different method of recording, retrieving, and selecting, and each system uses its own recording medium. An eight-track tape will not play in a cassette deck, and a CD will not play in an iPod.

When we are in a given situation, such as getting ready to step into a swimming pool, we have a reference level, R, for the "just right" state we want the water temperature to be. Where did that reference come from?

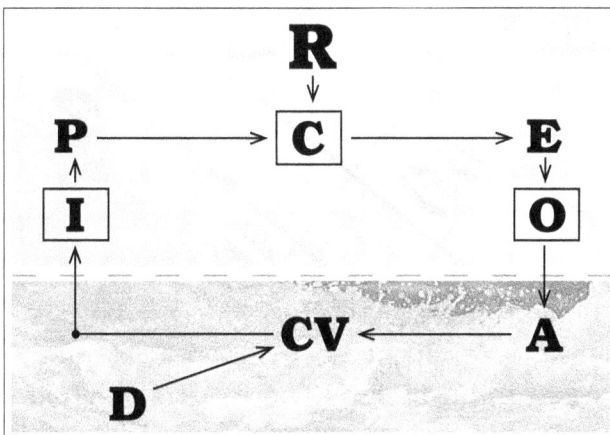

I'm getting ready to get into the pool, and I draw from a collection of "remembered perceptions" of water temperature for the one that is just right in this situation. If it is a really hot day, I may set a reference level for cool water. If it is cold outside, I may set a reference for warmer water. Both references come from my collection of remembered perceptions, my memory.

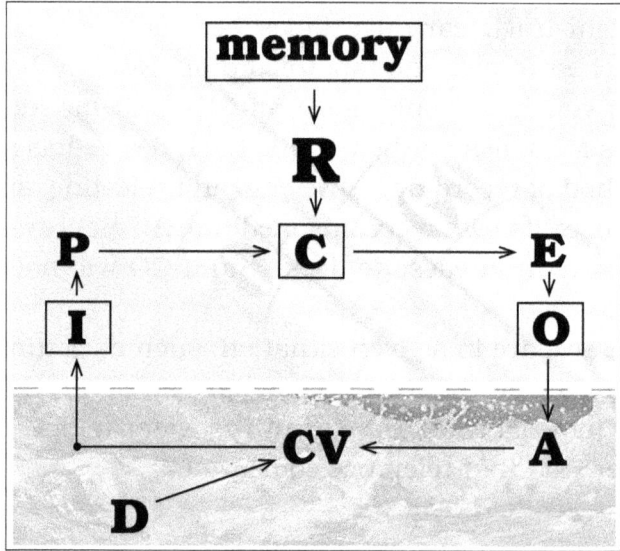

A reference signal is set from a collection of remembered perceptions at a higher level. Exactly how the system selects which reference isn't clear, but by placing memory in a box we know that it is a function, some computation occurs to select the reference at a given moment. Now we have one of the three elements of memory, an ability to select, and by attaching it to each individual loop, we have given it an address from which it can be retrieved. Remember that the output signal from the level above is transmitted through memory, and that the perceptual signal, P, from this level is transmitted out to the levels above.

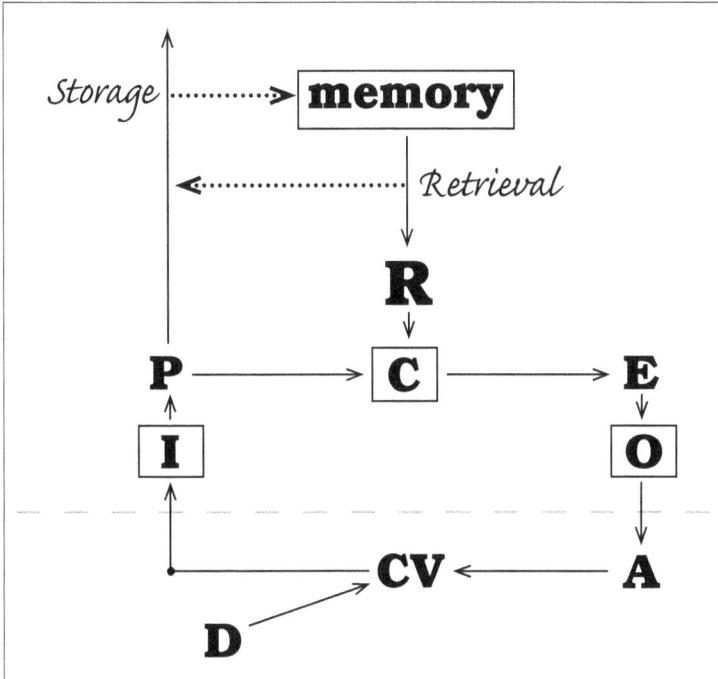

Take a minute to think about this diagram and the new elements added to it. Many signals enter the input function, I, and are converted to a single signal, a perceptual signal. This perceptual signal can go three different places: the comparator on this level, the memory on this level, and the input on the levels above. It's not clear whether every perception is being recorded. What is clear is that every single recorded perception is not being played back all of the time. Can you imagine the chaos if every "just right" water temperature you ever wanted was being played back simultaneously? Or if all the songs on an album were being played at once?

By placing memory in each loop, we know that different types of memory are stored in different places. Category perceptions, labels, and names are stored in the category level. Programs, algorithms, and sequences are stored at the program level, and so on.

This PCT explanation of memory allows us to have some order in the retrieval process. As Powers puts it, "Memory, in order to be useful, must be under control of some orderly addressing mechanism." Many researchers refer to this as addressing. If you have ever used memory pegs, a strategy for remembering bits of information that may or may not be connected, then you are familiar with using a scheme for storing information. One type of memory peg system involves visualizing a familiar place, like the rooms in your house, and then visualizing the bits of information you are trying to remember "hung up" on different objects in this familiar place. Another involves transposing numbers into visual images (1 is a flag pole, 2 is a swan, 3 is a two-hump camel), and then "hanging" the thoughts you are trying to remember on the number "pegs." For example, a person sitting on the top of a flag pole, the swan eating the state of Arizona, and a pitchfork digging out the space between the humps on the camel may help you remember that nouns are people, places, and things. There are very complex memory peg systems for remembering the periodic table of chemical elements. Anyone who has tried to find a document in his or her computer and can't remember where it was filed or what it was named understands the importance of organizing memory. Google (www.google.com) or Dogpile (www.dogpile.com) illustrate how retrieval of bits of information has become an entire industry. There is a strong correlation between how computers were originally designed and the PCT model. Much of what computers help us with is the storage and retrieval of bits of information, remembered perceptions. Whether they were conscious of it or not, the original developers of successful analog computers based them on models of human behavior.

In my workshops with teachers, we often do an activity whose goal is to give teachers a better understanding of how the brain works in the learning process. I give participants a bag full of marbles and a small container of play dough. I then ask them to work in small groups to construct three things, one using only marbles, one using only play dough, and one using both. While they are doing this activity, I ask them to record what they notice about the process and the products, how are they similar and how they are different. The groups can use nothing else to help them in their constructions, and they work on bare table tops. There are no tablecloths. Participants quickly find that the marbles, used alone, roll off the tables and on to the floor, and they always ask for something to contain the marbles. When groups work with play dough the task is easier, but the products are somewhat limited. The real fun comes from watching the groups as they do the third construction using both marbles and play dough. Many groups create entire stories about their creations.

The marbles represent random, lower level bits of information such as a name (*Madison is the capitol of Wisconsin*) or a mathematical fact (*2x2=4*) or a date (*Pearl Harbor was bombed on December 7, 1941*). As happens with the marbles, if there are no connections tying these lower level bits of information to higher level concepts and ideas (play dough), they roll right off the table and are lost. Based on how the hierarchy is developed, we know that higher level perceptions are made up of different combinations of lower level perceptions. This inexhaustible combining of lower level perceptions to create higher level perceptions creates a complex web of neural networks and yet allows for immense flexibility. By placing memory in the model of every loop, we show that there are different types of knowledge that are stored (recorded) and played back (retrieved) in different ways and at different levels.

Bill Powers explains the link between memory and learning this way: "All behavior consists of reproducing past

perceptions." Isn't that a big part of learning, especially in schools? We want the learner to reproduce a perception that we as the teachers believe demonstrates understanding. When Minnesota began implementing standards-based education, the state's campaign used the motto "Show What You Know." This idea aligns nicely with PCT. If I want someone to demonstrate the ability to dribble a basketball, I need to have them "show what they know" by reproducing the perception of dribbling a basketball, not by writing on a piece of paper. If I want a student to demonstrate an understanding of what 6x2 is, she could create two groups of six items each and count the items. She could write the answer on a piece of paper (12), or she could say the answer aloud, "twelve." Each of these methods would show me that she knows 6x2=12, that she has a remembered perception for this bit of knowledge. If I want someone to reproduce a perception, I need to ask them to reproduce it in the way that closely aligns to how it was stored.

If we want students to really learn something, it needs to be taught, practiced, and measured in the same way. To understand this, let's go back to the music systems we were talking about. If I want to play a vinyl record, I have to have a turntable, and I need to play it back using the same conditions under which it was recorded. I can't play a 45 RPM record at 33 1/3 RPM because it just won't sound "right." If I want to play something that was recorded on a cassette tape, I have to play it back on a cassette recorder. But in schools we often ask learners to play an MP3 file on a tape recorder. For example, show me that you know how to deliver an organized speech by writing an outline.

Before we become involved with students, we need to first ask ourselves what we want students to know and be able to do (what perceptions we want them to be able to reproduce). We then ask how we will measure their ability to reproduce that specific perception. (What evidence that they are able to control for a specific perception will we accept?) Next, ask how students can most effectively practice the learning (the more we use it or do it, the stronger the possibility is that it will be selected). In her book *Performance-Based Learning for the Multiple Intelligences Classroom*, Sally Berman provides an illustration:

> "Once upon a time, a school staff decided that its highest priority was helping students to become better writers. Students spent much time analyzing sentences to identify parts of speech. They combed through long lists of sentences looking for capitalization and punctuation errors. Exercising their visual skills, students diagramed sentences to show the relationships of the parts to the whole. Student investigators inspected sentences for subject/verb agreement, dangling participles, and split infinitives. At the end of the school year, students took a multiple–choice test to demonstrate their mastery of writing skills. Test scores were high. The school staff was pleased.
>
> Time passed. The students graduated and moved to new schools and jobs. One by one, they heard, 'You're writing is terrible! Where did you go to school? Didn't they teach you anything at that place? You need to take a remedial writing course if you want to be successful with us.' The students returned to the school exclaiming, 'We thought we were learning to write! But we don't know how to write! We just don't get it! You said you were teaching us how to write!'
>
> **The moral:** *Performing glues a skill in the brain; he (or she) who performs, learns.*

Marilee Sprenger gives a more technical explanation in *Learning & Memory: The Brain in Action* about how to enhance the process of selecting which perception to reproduce:

> "Researchers are currently exploring an important theory called *long-term potentiation.* LTP suggest that every time a neuron fires information across a synapse, the memory for that information is encoded exponentially. That means the information is learned multiple times each time it is practiced. The signal has changed the potential of the receiving neuron, and it now has the potential to learn faster."

The second type of learning Powers identifies is problem-solving programs, based on the idea that the brain is naturally designed to seek out and organize based on patterns. You've spent considerable time teaching with and teaching others how to use the *concept attainment* model of instruction, which is one type of problem-solving program. Probably the simplest way to explain concept attainment is to say that this type of learning is about sorting and categorizing. In *Models of Teaching*, Bruce Joyce and Marsha Weil describe this process in detail. The basic idea is to try to determine a category that was already formed in another person's mind, usually the teacher's. The teacher presents students with examples. Some incorporate all of the characteristics or attributes of the concept the teacher wants students to learn and others incorporate only a few or none of the characteristics or attributes. Using the process of pattern recognition the learner is presented with "right" and "wrong" perceptions and begins to sort and categorize lower level perceptions.

This is how you probably learned a lot of information

when you were a child. For example, when you began to identify vehicles, you probably called every vehicle on the road "car." When examples drove past that weren't cars and you said "car," your parents probably said, "No, that's a truck." Like most children, you probably had a puzzled look on your face and were trying to sort out internally why one moving object was a car and one a truck. Your parents didn't give a list of characteristics that define a truck and what distinguishes it from a car. If they had, you probably wouldn't have understood the words they were saying. Parents leave the attribute listing to you and your wonderful developing mind. They know that you can get the job done. Over time, you learned the attributes that differentiated a car from a truck. Joyce and Weil posit that understanding a concept means knowing all of its four elements: (1) name; (2) examples; (3) attributes (essential and nonessential): and (4) attribute values. *Attribute value* is how much of a "part" belongs with the "whole." In the vehicle example, all of the vehicles we talked about have wheels. In order for something to be considered not only a truck but a specific kind of a truck we call a "semi," it must not only have wheels, but it must also have eighteen of them. Attribute value defines the quantity of a specific attribute. Does the truck have enough wheels to be a semi? Does the vehicle have too many wheels to be a car? Children today who are trying to learn to categorize vehicles need to learn some subtle distinctions. When is something an SUV? When is it a truck? What is the difference between a suburban and a full-size SUV? Ask my son Duncan, and he can tell you, but cars aren't that important to me so I just haven't bothered to learn what I consider the subtle differences. According to Powers in *Behavior: The Control of Perception*, we don't just learn the category, but we learn "the means of categorizing the relevance or irrelevance of lower-order perceptions."

Thus concepts are made up of different combinations of lower level perceptions. A conceptual understanding of a topic is like play dough holding together random facts (or marbles). This type of learning occurs at the higher levels of the hierarchy. Just like giving workshop participants play dough to keep from "losing their marbles," helping students bump it up to conceptual learning helps them hold together the random bits of data they are asked to learn.

Now let's look at the third type of learning: reorganization. In some ways, the reorganizing system is the key to understanding behavior. Think of the reorganizing system as an overarching structure that monitors all parts of the system. It is a feedback loop on a mega level. Once you understand how feedback loops operate, you begin to see them everywhere, and like the Chinese nesting dolls, one loop can be subsumed as a component of a larger loop.

In the children's book *Zoom* by Istvan Banyai there's a picture of what appears to be an abstract drawing of a series of pointed red hills with designs drawn on them. On the next page, you see that the hills are really the cockscomb on a rooster. On the third page, you see that the rooster is just a part of a scene that two children are observing through an open window. Each picture is a component of a larger picture. In the same way, PCT starts with a simple loop, which is part of a more complex loop. The feedback loop is part of the hierarchy of control, which is made up of different levels. And the behavioral hierarchy, the levels of perception, are just a part of the reorganizing system. In PCT there is a close similarity among the whole and the parts. As in mathematics and in nature, there are wonderful examples of patterns within patterns. Take a look sometime at the fronds of a fern; a close look shows that the whole and the parts are not the same, but similar. A fern's frond is a small replica of the whole. The same is true of fractals in mathematics. So hang on to what you already know about the basic feedback loop. It will help you understand the reorganizing system, which is a closed negative feedback loop.

Think about the reorganizing system as a complete re-wiring. Reorganizing isn't about changing just one thing, like setting a different reference, wanting a specific TV sound level. Reorganization isn't about putting together a differ-ent combination of lower level loops, say to understand the difference between a car and a truck, or setting a reference for going to the store and then setting lower level references for keys, a grocery list, a car, backing out of the garage, and so on. Reorganization involves a more fundamental change that can shift the entire system.

I have discussed this idea before in terms of the first months of life. I talked about the idea that children go through fussy stages, clinging, crankiness, and crying, and that these are signals of major shifts in ability. Franz Plooij states "Apparently something fundamental is going on ten times in the first twenty months. We believe this something fundamental is the emergence of new types of control sys-tems with new types of perception and new types of learning instincts." This development of new types of control systems is what you might think of as learned behavior.

As we experience the world we learn to perceive and con-trol more and more of it. This is how the perceptual hier-archy of control is created. This hierarchy is fundamentally altered by the output of the reorganizing system. I can hear the screams now: "So everything you have talked about up to this point is only one part of a much larger loop?" Yup! It is a loop with one big difference: it is not directly affected by the environment. The reorganizing system is a closed loop and only deals directly with the intrinsic signals of the individual.

Think about the process of evolution. Ask yourself what creates the conditions for change in this process. In PCT

terms, the short answer is "mega ERROR!" The job of the reorganizing system is to reduce error in the organism. The process of reorganization is responsible for the development of the behavioral hierarchy, the levels of perception. The reorganizing system fundamentally changes the neurological system you were born with, probably by changing the synaptic thresholds via chemicals or neural signals or by creating new synaptic connections. This idea is very closely aligned to something I wrote earlier in this letter about the neuroscientist's definition of learning: "Neurons have 'learned' when one neuron sends a message to another neuron." Reorganization can re-wire parts of the neurological connections.

This is where genes probably play a role. In the behavioral hierarchy, reference signals come from the loops above (remembered perceptions). In the reorganizing system, reference signals are believed to come from *genetic sources*. So instead of labeling it R, we label it IR for *intrinsic reference signal*. The comparator (C) remains the same because its function is the same. The *intrinsic perceptual signal* is labeled IP. That means the *error signal* is also *intrinsic*, and is labeled IE. The input function in the reorganizing systems monitors *only* internal information. So any behavior produced by the behavioral hierarchy has two effects. One effect is sensory and alters the state of something in the environment that affects sensory endings. The other is physiological and alters the physiological state of the individual through physical and biochemical processes. As the physiological state of the individual changes based on activity such as eating, arousal, or illness, the input function monitors these neural and chemical changes and converts them into a single value, labeled the intrinsic perceptual signal, IP. Again, the input function acts as a record keeper, but this time it records the

Reorganizing System

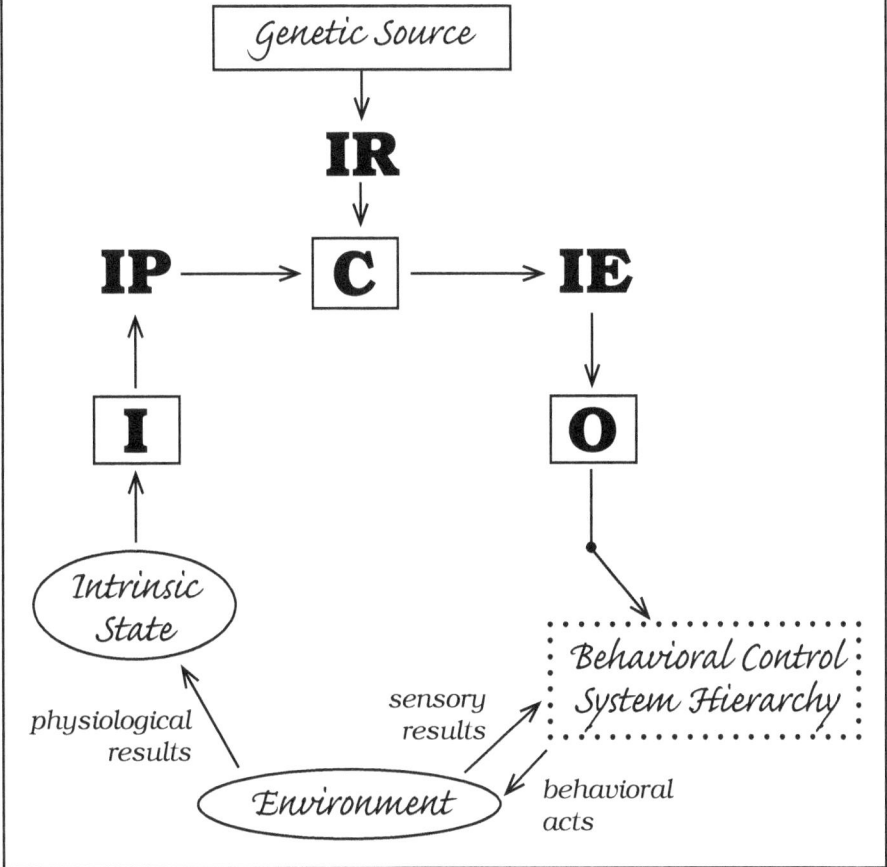

Genetic Source

IR

IP ———→ C ———→ IE

I

O

Intrinsic State

physiological results

sensory results

Behavioral Control System Hierarchy

Environment

behavioral acts

overall "state of wellness" of the individual. Powers believes this signal is compared to the intrinsic reference signal, IR, which is determined by genetics. As is the case with the behavioral system, when error approaches zero, the reorganizing system is not activated. When the difference varies too greatly from the genetically set range, the reorganizing system kicks into action. So what happens to the

output signals? They act on the behavioral hierarchy, not directly on the environment. Therefore, if behavior is reorganized, the hierarchy carries out its control activities in different ways, controlling new perceptual variables in new ways. The entire system gets re-wired.

Reorganization reminds me of my first year teaching algebra. Although I had been a fairly successful mathematician all through school, when I was faced with teaching algebra to a room full of eighth and ninth graders, I ran a lot of error. I would find myself thinking that something just didn't feel right. I was constantly uncomfortable. When I went to college, I thought that I was going to teach elementary students, and I thought that I understood mathematics far beyond the sixth grade level. That first year of teaching algebra, I think my behavioral hierarchy was involved in reorganization. I remember one time, about three-quarters of the way through the year, when I suddenly realized the real mathematical meaning of "function." At that moment, I wanted to go back and take calculus because much of what my calculus teachers had talked about would now make sense to me. This was not a moment when a single thing *came to light*. Rather, a whole lot of what I understood changed. We can't control the process of reorganization. We can't intentionally turn it on or off. The system starts acting in random ways to try to start "feeling" better when the intrinsic error signal becomes too great. As a principal, you have compared changing the workings of your elementary school with trying to change the tires on an airplane while it was flying. That was a good description of reorganization. This type of learning is not a nice, neat, logical, organized process. Like in nature, it happens in spurts, when it wants to, and it doesn't always make sense when viewed from the outside. As Phil Runkel says: "We need control loops to keep us alive, and we need the reorganizing system to adapt our

controlling to our unpredictable environment, but we cannot control our reorganizing system."

What does this have to do with learning and teaching? First, if there is no internal error, if a student doesn't want to learn something, then learning won't happen. Second, since we can't control reorganization, educators need to learn to recognize the teachable moments when reorganization is probably happening, when the learner doesn't "feel right" and is trying on new behaviors. There must be a difference between what the learner wants and what she is getting. That error can come from learned behaviors (the hierarchy) or some intrinsic sense that something isn't right. Third, if we can make learning more experiential to involve more of the lower levels, we have a better chance for learning to occur. We cannot assume that the lower level perceptions are there or that the student has the "correct" remembered perceptions. Learning is about re-creating a previous perceptual state, but something can't be re-created if it was never there in the first place. Many students have "holes" in their learning. Educators need to discover where students may have these, and go back and fill them in. Fourth, in order for students to learn to control for a specific perception, educators need to teach, practice, and assess in a way that is congruent. (We can't expect to listen to an MP3 file on a cassette player.)

To understand different types of learning in PCT terms, it helps to think in terms of computers. Storing a document I've created is one piece of learning. I can store the document, and when I need it again, I can go back and find it. It is easier for me to retrieve it if I know where to look for it. Think of document retrieval as long-term memory. Cutting and pasting is like short-term memory, I can use the information again right away, or I can put it into the system's clipboard for a longer period of time. But when I'm done

working and shut down the computer, that information is gone if I've not embedded it in a document. Problem-solving programs require the installation of software, which allow me to perform processes and tasks, like creating a spreadsheet for computation or sending messages via the Internet. Programs are a fixed list of instructions with decision-making points along the way. Reorganization completely changes the computers ability to perform. It's like changing the operating system in your computer, which dramatically changes the capabilities of your computer as a whole.

PCT has helped me understand the need for and importance of paying attention to what the learner already knows and what the learner wants to learn. The only way I know how to do that is to ask.

And there I go again. . . "Ask, don't tell!"

In a nutshell

- In PCT, there are three types of learning: memory, problem-solving programs, and reorganization.

- Memory is attached to each individual loop at all levels of the behavioral hierarchy.

- Virtually every behavior is the reproduction of a remembered perception.

- Problem-solving programs are based on the brains ability to seek patterns.

- Concept attainment is a learning process that involves learners creating a list of concept attributes that helps them distinguish it from other concepts (think cars and trucks).

- Isolated facts or random bits of data are like marbles to the brain, easily lost without something into which we can embed them.

- The behavioral hierarchy is one component of the reorganizing system.

- The intrinsic reference signals for the reorganizing system are thought to be genetic.

- The reorganizing system monitors the intrinsic state of the living system.

🖐 Reorganization is a random, uncontrollable process and continues until the intrinsic error nears zero.

🖐 It is important to know what the learner already knows and what the learner wants to learn.

🖐 Before teachers start planning how they are going to teach, they must know how they are going to measure learning. If we want students to really learn something, it needs to be taught, practiced, and measured in the same way.

CHAPTER 13

Dear Reader,

It's the

mind that

moves

There is a lesson in Buddhism about its sixth patriarch, Huineng. While traveling, he came across two monks arguing as they observed a flag. One monk said, "The flag is moving." The other disagreed and said, "The wind is moving." Huineng corrected them both by saying,

"Neither the wind nor the flag are moving. It is your mind that moves."

Dear Reader,

I hope this series of letters has helped you to better understand Perceptual Control Theory and think in some new and different ways. It's a lot to make sense of, so give yourself time to let these ideas percolate in your mind. Use the TLC process — Try it on, Let it go, Check it out — to make small changes.* (See the TLC worksheet on page 221.) Start with one skill-building idea and practice it until it becomes a habit. Ask more questions of yourself and others. Try to catch yourself when you make a statement, and see if you can turn it into a question. Or see if you can ask questions that get you further faster, shifting awareness higher up the levels of perception. Build on your strengths and slowly eliminate what you see as weaknesses.

My goal in writing this book is to help you better understand a fundamentally different way to think about behavior. As I've tried to deepen my own understanding of PCT, I've tried to keep in mind two things. First, keep it simple. (Think about how a plant lives rather than focusing on a more complex system, like a person.) Second, look to the model. For example, once I really understood feedback loops, a whole new world opened up for me. Even in the writing of this book, I reorganized my understanding of PCT. I now find that I can shift my awareness more easily because I am better able to realize when my reference doesn't match my perception. I know that what others say and do is *just information*, I remember to ask myself, *What's this all about?* when I'm struggling, seeking the reference until I don't need to ask it any longer. I focus on *bumping it up* and stop focusing on "the doing." I make connections when I know I'm going to be working with others, and I take the time to connect references at a higher level. I now ask more than I tell. When "dis" happens, my job is to figure out who I want to be. I know the only person I can control is me, and it's all about me. When I'm able to do this, I have less stress and can take more effective control of my life.

We as humans are complex living systems. Like other living systems, we have internal "just right" conditions that we try to match. All behavior is about controlling for a match between a perception (the present state as it is recorded) and a reference (the ideal state we want at that moment). The actions we take are intended to reduce the difference (error) between the two. PCT explains that behavior is all about relationships — the relationship between the reference and the perception, the relationship between the environment and ourselves, the relationship between the results of our actions and our perception, and a whole lot of other relationships. One piece of data isn't enough to give us an understanding of what we observe. Although the basic feedback loop that diagrams the process of control is simple, the behavioral hierarchy is an intricate web of interconnected loops that grows and changes with experience.

As you learn more about PCT and help others learn, remember that motivation comes from *error*, a mismatch between a want and a have. Motivation comes not from the want of the teacher, but from the want of the student. Also remember that when we learn, we are going to make mistakes. The highest form of learning, reorganization, is riddled with random acts and lots of error.

If you are a parent, when in conflict with your children, try to remember to reduce your own error first. Take the time to make an agreement as a family to connect references on the kind of family you want to be. Model the behaviors you most want your children to practice. And don't forget to ask, ask, ask!

If you are a manager, understand that organizations are made up of individuals, and change happens one person at a time, often in baby steps. Help your employees self-evaluate, and remember that no matter what business you are in, you are in the people business.

To those of you in the helping professions, ask yourselves the question Bill Powers often asks, "What does it mean to help someone?" My answer would be the same as Tim Carey's in his book *Method of Levels*: "Get out of the way." As a helper, all I can do is ask you to examine your own thinking and your references at higher and higher levels.

To those of you who have the energy of youth on your

side, and for those of you who have a wealth of life experiences, I hope you have learned to take more effective control of your own life. How you perceive the world around you has a profound impact. Make an agreement with yourself about the person you want to be, and end each day asking, "In what ways was I the person I wanted to be today?"

I encourage you to evaluate yourself more and evaluate others less. Remember this book is all about you! It is about your truth, your relationships with others, and most importantly your relationship with yourself! And finally, I hope you've enjoyed meeting my friends, the recipients of these letters. Each of them in his or her own way has been my teacher, and teaching is the greatest gift you can give the world.

I hope you've learned a lot!

PCT in a nutshell

Mottoes to integrate PCT principles into your life.

- Remember it's all about you! You can only control yourself.

- Recognize it's just information.

- Seek the reference.

- Connect references at the higher levels.

- Pull, don't push.

- Ask, don't tell.

- Bump it up!

- Reduce self-error first.

- Live in the present.

- Who holds the bag of truth?

- It's OK to make a mistake.

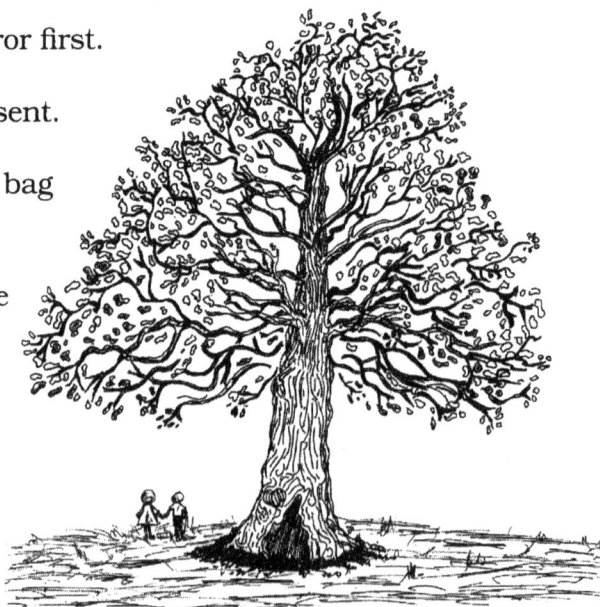

Illustration by Rick Watlington

220

Try it on...

What are a few things you want to try to do differently?

Let it go...

What are a few things (thinking and actions) you are willing to let go of?

Check it out...

After you try it on for a few days, come back and reflect on what difference it made.

For further reading . . .

Arntz, William, Betsy Chasse, and Mark Vincente. *What the Bleep Do We Know!?: Discovering the Endless Possibilities for Altering Your Everyday Reality*. Health Communications, 2005.

Banyai, Istvan, *Zoom*. Pufffin Books, 1995.

Beckhard, Richard, and Reuben T. Harris. *Organizational Transitions: Managing Complex Change*. Addison-Wesley Publishing Co., 1987.

Berman, Sally, *Performance Based Learning for the Multiple Intelligences Classroom*. Skylight Professional Development, 1999.

Boffey, D. Barnes. *My Gift in Return: Thoughts on the Journey to Becoming Real*. New View Publications, 2003.

Booth Sweeny, Linda. *When a Butterfly Sneezes: A Guide for Helping Kids Explore Interconnections in Our World Through Favorite Stories*. Pegasus Communications, 2001

Bridges, William. *Transitions: Making Sense of Life's Changes*. Addison-Wesley Publishing Co., 1990.

Capra, Fritjof. *The Web of Life: A New Scientific Understanding of Living Systems*. First Anchor Books, 1996.

Carey, Timothy A. *The Method of Levels; How to Do Psychotherapy Without Getting in the Way*. Living Control Systems Publishing, 2006

Chaiklin, Seth. "The Zone of Proximal Development in Vygotsky's Analysis of Learning and Instruction." In *Vygotsky's Educational Theory in Cultural Context*. Edited by Alex Kozulin, Boris Gindis, Vladimir S. Ageyev, and Suzanne M. Miller. Cambridge University Press, 2003.

Chaline, Eric. *The Book of Zen: The Path to Inner Peace*. Barron's Educational Series, 2003.

FURTHER READING

Coelho, Paulo. Translated by Alan R. Clarke. *The Valkyries.* HarperCollins, 1996

Cornelius, Helena, and Shoshana Faire. *Everyone Can Win: How to Resolve Conflict.* Simon & Schuster, 1989.

Covey, Stephen R. *The Seven Habits of Highly Effective People: Restoring the Character Ethic.* Simon & Schuster, 1989.

Csikszentmihalyi, Mihaly. *Flow: The Psychology of Optimal Experience.* HarperCollins, 1991.

DuFour, Richard, Rebecca DuFour, and Robert Eaker. *On Common Ground: The Power of Professional Learning Communities.* National Education Services, 2005.

Emmons, Henry, and Rachel Kranz, *The Chemistry of Joy: A Three-step Program for Overcoming Depression Through Western Science and Eastern Wisdom.* Simon & Schuster, 2006.

Forssell, Dag. *Management and Leadership: Insight for Effective Practice.* Living Control Systems Publishing, 2005.

Good, E. Perry, Jeff Grumley, and Shelley Roy. *A Connected School.* New View Publishing, 2003.

Greenfield, Susan A. *The Human Brain: A Guided Tour.* Basic Books, 1997.

Hanh, Thich Nhat. *The Art of Mindful Living: How to Bring Love, Compassion, and Inner Peace into Your Daily Life.* (Audiobook) Sounds True, 2000.

Hayward, Jeremy W. *Letters to Vanessa: On Love, Science, and Awareness in an Enchanted World.* Shambhala Publications, 1997.

Jensen, Eric. *Completing the Puzzle: The Brain-Based Approach to Learning.* Turning Point Publishing, 1996.

Jampolsky, Gerald G., and Diane V. Cirincione. *Love is the Answer: Creating Positive Relationships.* Random House, 1991.

Joyce, Bruce, and Marsha Weil. *Models of Teaching.* Prentice-Hall, 1986.

Kanter, Rosabeth Moss. *The Change Masters: Corporate Entrepreneurs at Work.* Taylor & Francis, 1990.

Kuhn, Thomas S. *The Structure of Scientific Revolutions*. University of Chicago Press, 1962.

Marken, Richard S. *More Mind Readings: Methods and Models in the Study of Purpose*. newview publications, 2002.

Marx, Jeffrey. Season of Life: A Football Star, a Boy, a Journey to Manhood. Simon & Schuster, 2003.

McClelland, Kent A., and Thomas J. Fararo. *Purpose, Meaning, And Action: Control Systems Theories in Sociology*. Palgrave McMillian, 2006.

Miller, Sherod, Daniel B. Wackman, Dallas R. Demmitt, and Nancy J. Demmitt. *Working Together: Productive Communication on the Job*. Interpersonal Communication Programs, 1985.

Nagao, Tadahiko and Isamu Saito. *Kokology: The Game of Self-Discovery*. Simon and Schuster, 2000.

Nerburn, Kent. *Small Graces: The Quiet Gifts of Everyday Life*. New World Library, 1998.

Peacock, Fletcher. *Water the Flowers Not The Weeds*. Montreal, Quebec; Open Heart Publishing, 2000.

Powers, William T. *Behavior: The Control of Perception*, Aldine Publishing Company, 1973.

Powers, William T. *Making Sense of Behavior: The Meaning of Control*. Benchmark Publications, 1998.

Powers, William T. *Living Control Systems; Selected Papers of William T. Powers*. Control System Group, 1989.

Powers, William T., and Richard J. Robertson. *Introduction to Modern Psychology: The Control-Theory View*. The Control System Group, 1990.

Radin, Dean. *Entangled Minds: Extrasensory Experiences in a Quantum Reality*. Paraview, 2006.

Runkel, Philip J., People as Living Things: The Psychology of Perceptual Control Theory. Living Control Systems Publishing, 2003.

Satinover, Jeffrey. *The Quantum Brain: The Search for Freedom and the Next Generation of Man*. John Wiley & Sons, 2001.

FURTHER READING

Senge, Peter, Richard Boss, Bryan Smith, Charlotte Roberts, and Art Kleiner. *The Fifth Discipline Fieldbook: Strategies and Tools for Building a Learning Organization.* Doubleday, 1994.

Shapiro, Andrea. *Creating Contagious Commitment: Applying the Tipping Point to Organizational Change.* Strategy Perspective, 2003

Soldani, James, "Effective Personnel Management: An Application of Perceptual Control Theory." in *Volitional Action: Conation and Control* edited by W.A. Hershberger. North-Holland, 1989.

Sprenger, Marilee. *Learning and Memory: The Brain in Action.* Association for Supervision and Curriculum Development, 1999.

Vanderijt, Hetty, and Frans X. Plooij. *The Wonder Weeks: How to Turn Your Baby's 8 Great Fussy Phases into Magical Leaps Forward.* Rodale, 2003.

Vygotsky, Lev S. *Mind in Society: The Development of Higher Psychological Processes.* Harvard University Press, 1978.

Wheatley, Margaret J. *Leadership and the New Science: Discovering Order in a Chaotic World.* Berrett-Koehler Publishers, 1999.

Weisbord, Marvin Ross. *Productive Workplaces; Organizing and Managing for Dignity, Meaning, and Community.* Jossey-Bass, 1991.

About the Author

Shelley A.W. Roy is president of Synergy Transition Consulting. A recognized leader in human resource development, Shelley has worked with thousands of adults in a wide range of learning situations. For more than ten years, she provided facilitation to more than seventy improvement teams and several multi-agency collaboratives. She has taught in the K-12 system and at the university level in West Berlin, Germany; The Navajo Reservation, Tohatchi, New Mexico; Junction City, Kansas; Leigh, Nebraska; and St. Cloud, Minnesota. In her workshops and seminars across the United States and internationally, she shares the latest in leadership, human behavior, effective communication, brain compatible instruction, change management and team building. Shelley has written *A Connected School* (New View Publications, 2003) with co-authors Perry Good ad Jeff Grumley. She lives in Sartell, Minnesota, with her two sons.

www.ingramcontent.com/pod-product-compliance
Lightning Source LLC
Chambersburg PA
CBHW070802280326
41934CB00012B/3017